MEDICINE & HEALTH
THROUGH TIME

TEACHERS' RESOURCE BOOK

SHP provision for GCSE and Standard Grade

DEPTH STUDIES for SHP specifications

- **The American West 1840–1895**   Students' Book   0 7195 5181 1
        Teachers' Book   0 7195 5182 X

- **Britain 1815–1851**   Students' Book   0 7195 7478 1
        Teachers' Book   0 7195 7479 X

- **Elizabethan England**   Students' Book   0 7195 7474 9
        Teachers' Book   0 7195 7475 7

- **Germany 1918–1945**   Students' Book   0 7195 7059 X
        Teachers' Book   0 7195 7220 7

- **South Africa 1948–1994**   Students' Book   0 7195 7476 5
        Teachers' Book   0 7195 7477 3

DEVELOPMENT STUDIES for SHP specifications

- **Crime & Punishment through Time**   Students' Book   0 7195 5261 3
        Teachers' Book   0 7195 5262 1

- **Medicine & Health through Time**   Students' Book   0 7195 5265 6
        Teachers' Book   0 7195 5266 4

- **Essential Medicine & Health through Time**   Students' Book   0 7195 8537 6
        Teachers' Book   0 7195 8538 4

MODERN WORLD STUDIES for SHP specifications

- **The Struggle for Peace in Northern Ireland**   Students' Book   0 7195 7472 2
        Teachers' Book   0 7195 7473 0

DEPTH STUDIES for Modern World History specifications or Standard Grade

- **Britain & the Great War (Revised Edition for GCSE)**   Students' Book   0 7195 7347 5

- **Germany 1918–1945**   Students' Book   0 7195 7059 X
        Teachers' Book   0 7195 7220 7

- **Russia & the USSR 1905–1941**   Students' Book   0 7195 5255 9
        Teachers' Book   0 7195 5256 7

- **South Africa 1948–1994**   Students' Book   0 7195 7476 5
        Teachers' Book   0 7195 7477 3

- **The USA between the Wars 1919–1941**   Students' Book   0 7195 5259 1
        Teachers' Book   0 7195 5260 5

THE SCHOOLS HISTORY PROJECT
S·H·P
SCHOOLS HISTORY PROJECT
OFFICIAL TEXT

DISCOVERING THE PAST FOR GCSE

IAN DAWSON

IAN COULSON

Medicine & Health THROUGH TIME

Teachers' resource book

Series Editor: Colin Shephard

JOHN MURRAY

Acknowledgments

p. 80 *t* © The Trustee of the Wellcome Trust, *b* Copyright British Museum; **p. 81 and p.144** *tl* The Mansell Collection; **p.88** National Library of Jamaica; **p.91 and p.144** *br* Hulton Getty Collection; **p.97** Bridgeman Art Library, London, Royal College of Surgeons, London; **p.105 and p.107** *t* The Mansell Collection; **p.107** Punch; **p.141** *tr* Reproduced by kind permission of The Royal College of Physicians, London, *l* Mary Evans Picture Library, *r* © Institut Pasteur, Paris, *bl* The Mansell Collection, *br* The Mansell Collection; **p. 143** *tl* Mary Evans Picture Library, *tr* The Mansell Collection, *r* Ann Ronan Picture Library, *b* Wellcome Institute Library; **p.144** *br* Mary Evans Picture Library.

(*t* = top, *b* = bottom, *r* = right, *l* = left)

Note: The wording and sentence structure of some written sources have been adapted and simpli ed to make them accessible to all students, while faithfully preserving the sense of the original.

Series consultants
Terry Fiehn
Tim Lomas
Martin and Jenny Tucker

© Ian Dawson and Ian Coulson 1997

First published in 1997
by John Murray (Publishers) Ltd., a member of the Hodder Headline Group
338 Euston Road
London NW1 3BH

Reprinted 1998, 1999, 2001 (twice), 2002 (twice), 2003

Layouts by Can Do Design
Artwork by Art Construction, Karen Donnelly, Philip Ford, Mike Humphries, Linden Artists, and Steve Smith
Typeset in 10½/12 pt Walbaum Book by Wearset, Boldon, Tyne & Wear
Printed and bound by Selwood Printing Ltd, West Sussex

A catalogue entry for this book is available from the British Library

ISBN 0-7195-5266-4
Students' Book 0-7195-5265-6

$\mathbf{C}$ontents

Introduction   1

About the series   1
The Schools History Project   1
Medicine and Health Through Time   2
    Aims   2
    Structure   2
    Organising your course   2
    Support materials   2
    Using the material in the classroom   2
    Differentiation   3
    Learning trouble spots   4
    Timelines   4

Detailed teachers' notes   5

Introduction   5
Chapter 1: From prehistory to the empires of Egypt, Greece and Rome 3000BC–AD500   7
Chapter 2: Medicine and health AD500–1400   14
Chapter 3: Medicine and health 1400–1750   17
Chapter 4: Medicine and health 1750–1900   20
Chapter 5: Medicine and health in the twentieth century   26
Chapter 6: Conclusions: explaining change and continuity in medicine and health   30

Photocopiable worksheets for: 34

Students' Book Introduction   34
Students' Book Chapter 1   39
Students' Book Chapter 2   63
Students' Book Chapter 3   69
Students' Book Chapter 4   76
Students' Book Chapter 5   113
Students' Book Chapter 6   136

Appendix: Using this Teachers' Resource Book alongside Medicine for Edexcel 151

Introduction

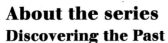

About the series

Discovering the Past

Series Editor: Colin Shephard (formerly Director of SHP)

Discovering the Past for GCSE

Discovering the Past is the Schools History Project's series of course books and teachers' books for Key Stage 3, GCSE and A level history.

At GCSE level, *Discovering the Past* resources both SHP GCSE syllabuses and Modern World History. A list of titles in the GCSE series can be found at the beginning of this book.

Coherence across the key stages

Discovering the Past has become the most widely used history course at Key Stage 3. It has greatly affected teaching methods in Y7–Y9 through its core text books, option units, Special Needs Support Material, and INSET support for all aspects of history teaching and learning. *Discovering the Past for GCSE* deliberately follows many of the precedents of the Key Stage 3 books and allows users of the Key Stage 3 books to continue with similar teaching approaches.

Exam requirements

At the same time the series has adapted those techniques to suit the requirements of exam preparation. The series has been conceived, written and edited by individuals who are closely involved in GCSE examining as chief examiners, assistant examiners and moderators. The needs of students to revise content effectively, to develop their skills in extended writing, to complete course work assignments, to express themselves effectively have been an integral part of the planning and writing of the books in the series.

■ An issue-based approach

Issues and questions raised by the content give each unit its identity. These genuine historical issues and controversies encourage students to question conventional interpretations of the past.

■ The role of the individual

By focusing on case studies of particular places and individuals, the series avoids historical stereotypes. Instead, students can begin to appreciate the variety and complexity of a period.

■ Classroom appeal

The series uses the best classroom practices, combining innovation and familiar techniques to ensure variety for the student and the teacher. A range of readers, advisers and trialling schools have ensured the classroom appeal of the material across the Key Stages.

■ Special Needs Support

Special Needs Support Material is available for each of the statutory units in Key Stage 3 and is planned for various GCSE units.

■ Source-based learning

The student tasks and enquiries use a wide range of source material – so that source-based work is thoroughly integrated into work on historical understanding.

■ Enquiry and communication

The series offers a wide range of exercises that allow students to present their historical findings in extended writing, using a variety of techniques such as reports, essays, diaries, leaflets, letters or articles.

THE SCHOOLS HISTORY PROJECT

This project was set up by the Schools Council in 1972. Its main aim was to suggest suitable objectives for history teachers, and to promote the use of appropriate materials and teaching methods for their realisation. This involved a reconsideration of the nature of History and its relevance in secondary schools, the design of a syllabus framework which shows the uses of History in the teaching of adolescents, and the setting up of appropriate examinations.

Since 1978 the project has been based at Trinity and All Saints' College, Leeds. It is now self-funding and with the advent of the National Curriculum it has expanded its publications to provide courses throughout Key Stages 1–3, and for a range of GCSE and A level syllabuses. The project provides INSET for all aspects of National Curriculum, GCSE and A level history, and also publishes *Discoveries*, a journal for History teachers.

Enquiries about the project, INSET and *Discoveries* should be addressed to the Schools History Project, Trinity and All Saints' College, Brownberrie Lane, Horsforth, Leeds LS18 5HD.

Enquiries about the *Discovering the Past* series should be addressed to the publishers, John Murray.

Series consultants

Terry Fiehn
Tim Lomas
Martin and Jenny Tucker

Medicine and Health Through Time

Aims

Medicine and Health Through Time can be a fascinating course. It has long been the most popular development study in SHP. However, it has also posed many teaching problems. This book aims to provide an innovative approach to the unit to solve some of the problems which students have faced in the past, and to supply a fresh and challenging approach for teachers who may have been using the same teaching material for many years.

Our aims have therefore been to:

■ provide an interesting and motivating course for students and teachers
■ provide thorough exam preparation for all medicine syllabuses
■ package the conceptually difficult areas of the syllabus more effectively than earlier books have done, e.g. to ensure that students can maintain their overview of the content at the same time as tackling certain topics in depth
■ develop students' ability to do the work of an historian: to organise their historical ideas and findings, to ask their own questions, to collect and record information and to present their results using a range of different techniques.

Structure

Chapters 1–5 of *Medicine & Health Through Time* Students' Book investigate continuities and changes in the history of medicine and health through six different periods:

prehistory (Chapter 1)
ancient civilisations (Chapter 1)
the Middle Ages (Chapter 2)
the Medical Renaissance (Chapter 3)
the nineteenth century (Chapter 4)
the twentieth century (Chapter 5)

Our study of each period is based around a number of generic questions which are applied to each period:

What made people healthy or unhealthy?
What ideas did people have about the causes of disease?
What kinds of treatments did they use?
Who provided medical care?
What caused continuity or change in medicine in this period?
How healthy were ordinary people and how were they affected by medical progress?

These questions have determined our choice of case studies although there has also been a conscious attempt to vary the approach from chapter to chapter.

Chapter 6 reviews the chronological content but through a conceptual framework investigating patterns of change and factors affecting change.

Among the other requirements which have driven this book are to allow students to study:

the role of key individuals in the history of medicine
the importance of different causal factors – and how those factors varied in importance at different times
the broad patterns of change and continuity

Organising your course

Because we have attempted to cover the requirements of a range of syllabuses there is clearly more in this book than you will be able to use in any one GCSE course.

Your approach to teaching this unit and your selection of what to cover will have to be based on the requirements of your own syllabus. We cannot go into the distinctive requirements of each syllabus here, but they vary in content, focus, case studies and assessment arrangements. Be sure to start with the requirements and objectives of your own group's syllabus. This book is particularly closely geared to the content and assessment requirements of the Midland Examining Group's syllabus.

Support materials

The questions and activities in the Students' Book are designed to be accessible to all abilities, and the worksheets in this book give further support in the form of writing frames, grids, and essay structures. The detailed notes from page 5 onwards also suggest alternative teaching strategies which may help weaker students.

Using the material in the classroom

The book is split into a number of discrete enquiries. Some are short (a single page) others – particularly those which are tackling the central concerns of the syllabus – are much longer and might provide for a few weeks' work. In these longer enquiries there are usually a number of tasks *en route* and then a major piece of work at the end (in a blue ruled box).

The questions and discussions during the rest of the enquiry are an important part of the process of getting ready to tackle these summary tasks.

The main purpose of the summary tasks is to show how students have brought together a range of skills and understanding. However, they are also crucial for exam preparation. Many will give invaluable experience in both recalling and organising knowledge but also in creating a bank of work students can use for revision.

Before starting out on an enquiry always read the questions and activities in the Students' Book and the descriptions and suggestions in this Teachers' Book in the detailed notes on pages 5–33. Make sure the students know the ultimate aims of the enquiry or of any piece of work they are undertaking.

A lot of tasks require group work, and many suggest the use of display or presentations. All these have implications for how you organise your classroom.

Sources are an integral part of the book – some spreads consist of almost nothing but sources. They are designed to be used; many of the questions within an enquiry are designed to ensure that students read, study and understand the source material provided, acquiring source-evaluation skills in the process.

Consistent with our aim of providing useful learning experiences for the students, we have translated, simplified and edited written source material to make it accessible. Make it clear to students that spelling and punctuation have been made contemporary. Modern equivalent words have been substituted where necessary, or definitions provided. Major edits have usually been shown by ellipses. However, the sense and meaning of all sources have been preserved.

The source line – which introduces and describes the source being studied – is an important tool for the student. It contains the details that students will need to know to answer any questions, such as who made or wrote the source and when. Encourage students to see these source lines as an important part of the evidence.

In most questions the reasons students give for their answers are as important as the answers themselves. In explaining why they have answered in a certain way they will reveal how deeply they have understood an issue. We have not, however, constantly reiterated in the questions 'explain your answer', as it gets highly repetitive. Students at GCSE level should be well aware that all historical answers require backing up by evidence. However, you might want to remind students of this more often than we have done.

Differentiation

First-hand classroom experience of teaching from SHP's *Discovering the Past* series has made it clear that students of all abilities can tackle the type of questions and issues in this book, *provided that they are not overwhelmed by being given too many sources, and that the sources they do use are of a suitable level of difficulty.*

One successful approach with mixed ability classes is to have all students attempting the same tasks but to reduce the amount of source material for some of them. This can be done in a number of ways:

- You can divide the class into groups and ask each group to consider just one or two sources. The groups' findings can then be pooled.
- Some groups can use just one source and others can use all the sources. This can be quite successfully done if the groups are carefully selected.
- Instead of splitting the class into groups you can, with careful class management, give individual students different amounts of source material to use.

As a general principle, as soon as it becomes clear that a student is finding a task difficult, the amount of material he/she is asked to use should be reduced. The important principle remains, however, that all students are being posed the same questions, even if the amount of source material they are using is varied.

Strategies such as these should ensure that all students end up succeeding (at their own level) with each of the tasks in the book.

It is also important that students are not left alone to tackle each enquiry. The book has been written with the expectation that much of the material in the authors' text will be introduced by the teacher. It might be that the teacher reads a spread through beforehand and then uses the information it provides to set the scene for students before they proceed to the sources and questions.

It is also sound practice to read and discuss all sources with students. We are attempting to develop students' skills and understanding, which will not be achieved by simply leaving them to get on with the questions by themselves all the time.

Group work can also help here. Some students will contribute to small group discussion, and risk putting forward ideas and answers, in a way which they would not do in front of the whole class. We have all seen how students tend to experiment more in small groups, partly because they are not so worried about getting things wrong.

In this course students are working with new content, ideas, skills and problems for much of the time and we should not be surprised if their early attempts to answer a question fall well below what might be regarded as a good answer. However, any genuine attempts to tackle the questions should be encouraged – the teacher can then begin to suggest how such answers could be built on. If students are worried about 'getting it wrong' they will play safe and their progress will be hindered.

Learning trouble spots

It pays to be aware in advance of areas of the course which weaker students sometimes find particularly daunting:

- chronology: the sequencing of societies and the overlaps among early societies
- that societies could hold more than one theory about the cause of disease
- that people in the past regularly used treatments that today seem illogical

- scientific developments, e.g. germ theory or other theories about the cause of disease, e.g. the theory of the four humours.

We have provided particular support for tackling these areas as follows:

- by focusing investigations on these problems; or
- by providing supportive material among these worksheets; or
- by presenting these ideas as clearly as possible and in a variety of styles.

Timelines

In a course with such a broad chronological sweep the use of class timelines will be very important. One of the challenges of the Medicine course is 'to see the wood for the trees'. The use of timelines and other devices to contextualise students' in-depth work on a period will be very useful. At the start of the course cover one wall with a 5000-year timeline, another with a large-scale timeline of whatever period you are studying at that time. Use the families on page 34 to characterise each period. Display them on the timeline. Display students' work at appropriate points on the timeline.

Detailed teachers' notes

I*ntroduction*

Enquiry: Health care today: has it always been like this?

Students' Book pp. 2–3

Taken together, pages 2–6 introduce the major themes and issues of this development study. Getting the pace of work right for each class will be vital. Students may well feel impatient with the role of an introduction and want to move on to the 'real work' of Chapter 1. However, they will make more sense of Chapter 1 if they understand how it fits into the whole development study.

The main purpose of pages 2–3 is to start students thinking about patterns of change and continuity in the history of medicine by completing the **Activity** on page 3. One approach is to begin with the knowledge in students' heads rather than on the page. Ask students first to make the two lists in the Activity (either in pairs or as a whole class) from their own knowledge and experience, and then secondly to supplement those lists using the text on pages 2–3. This will give you some idea of the extent of students' medical knowledge and vocabulary and, if they come up with good lists of their own, may enhance their confidence for dealing with this whole topic.

Having constructed the lists, the main value of the exercise is to find out which people/ treatments/methods were in use 100 and 1000 years ago. Transfer this information quickly onto a rough timeline on the board and then see what answers are forthcoming to questions such as:

- Have medical treatments and methods always been the same?
- How much change has there been in the last 100 years?
- How much change was there before the last 100 years?
- Why do you think there has been so much change in the last 100 years?
- How do you think this pattern has affected how long people have lived?

These issues need clarity and pace rather than a slow poring over of detail. Emphasise that these are the kinds of question that will be revisited during the development study. The chief value of

written work at this stage would be to note some of the first ideas which students can look back on later, particularly in answer to two questions:

- When was the time of greatest change in medicine?
- Why do you think there was great change then?

Enquiry: What is a development study?

Students' Book pp. 4–6
Worksheets 1, 2, 3, 4

The three elements on pages 4–5 are again intended to start students thinking briefly about issues rather than spending lengthy chunks of time constructing perfect answers.

(Pages 4–5)
Source 1 on page 4 links back to some of the questions suggested above for pages 2–3, i.e. about patterns of change and continuity and about life expectancies. The main purpose is to emphasise that they will be investigating a broad sweep of history and will find out why those life expectancies were:

- so similar for so long; and
- why they then changed so rapidly.

Although the average life expectancy figures on page 4 are broadly accurate, they should be approached with some caution in view of the many different ways of measuring that are used. Some reflect age at death; some average out including infant deaths; some exclude infant deaths and some are life expectancy of adults who have achieved a given age.

Causes of illness
Source 2 gives you the chance to explain that students will not just be working on the technology of medicine and health but also on the ideas that people had – both doctors and ordinary people. Before looking at this it would be worth asking students to write down their own explanations of why people become sick. Can they use words like bacteria or germ? How would they prove this was the true cause of sickness?

Then ask students to suggest which groups had which ideas, possibly undertaking a matching exercise using the pictures in **Worksheets 1 and 2**. This could be done in pairs or threes, the results compared, and the answers entered on **Worksheet 4**.

Two alternatives to then providing the right answers yourself are:

■ Set a research homework asking students to comb through the book to find out whether their answers were right.
■ Put the class's or each group's answers on the wall (perhaps using blow-ups of Worksheets 1 and 2) and check them off as you work through the development study. Who got them right in the first place?

Methods of treating illness

Source 3: Question 3 can be left open or be highly structured, depending on the ability level of the class/groups. To structure the task ask students to focus on one or two of the methods in turn, suggesting which healers might have used them. They could be tackled in the following order, working from the method to the healer:

■ the tablet
■ cutting out the infection
■ clearing away dirt
■ praying to God
■ charm with magic powers
■ herbal potions
■ drilling a hole
■ balancing the humours.

It needs to be emphasised that some of the methods could be used by more than one healer. Again, a matching exercise could be undertaken using the material in **Worksheets 1–3** cut up so that the pieces can be moved around. The answers can also be entered on Worksheet 4 to summarise conclusions.

(Page 6)
Factors causing change

Page 6 introduces the factors that explain changes and continuities in the history of medicine. This again links back to questions raised in relation to the Activity on page 3. Writing down the factors and these examples in the back of exercise books will help to establish the factors in students' minds. Later, students will be able to add more examples of the impact of these factors to their grid – these are listed below in the notes.

As part of the initial testing of ideas, you could ask students which factor(s) they think have been the most important in the history of medicine and then construct a league table of factors – the most important at the top – on the wall which could then be considered and altered as the study programme progresses.

Additional resource

A fascinating account of trephining, and of a healer using aboriginal methods, can be found in Gillian Cross' novel for children, *Born of the Sun* (Mammoth paperback 1995; OUP 1983). Chapters 19-21 contain the main medical passages based, according to the author's note, on passages from Ross Salmon's *My Quest for El Dorado*, describing a visit to such a healer in South America in 1977. Unfortunately, the authors have not yet been able to find Salmon's book.

Chapter 1: From prehistory to the empires of Egypt, Greece and Rome 3000BC–AD500

Page 7 introduces the chronological span from prehistory to the Romans and can be used as a stimulus page, comparing the pictures of the prehistoric and Roman families. Oral questions could be focused on:

- what kinds of treatments they used
- how their living conditions affected their health
- whether their healers understood what caused illness
- why some Roman families lived longer lives
- why students think there might have been medical progress in this period.

Enquiry: How healthy were people in prehistoric Britain?

Students' Book pp. 8–13
Worksheets 5, 6, 7, 8

Pages 8–10 introduce prehistoric medicine and health by using a specific site and people rather than simply generalising about the period. The text on page 8 telling of the discovery of the site has more impact if told as a story to students before the Activity and evidence are introduced.

The Tomb of the Eagles at Isbister, Orkney, 3000BC

Activity: This cannot all be completed from the evidence on pages 8–9. That is part of the objective. Students can complete the first two rows of **Worksheet 5** or a chart in their own exercise books. The kinds of answers they could provide are shown on page 10 but the fact that they are there should be kept secret from students if possible! An alternative way of presenting the evidence is to photocopy **Worksheet 6**, cut it up and put the pieces in envelopes; then give each individual or group of students an envelope, in the style of the 'What is History?' Mark Pullen exercise.

This exercise therefore has two objectives:

- to acquire knowledge of health and health problems; and
- to show students that archaeological evidence does not answer all our questions and therefore we need to look elsewhere for the answers.

For teachers still struggling to measure heights in centimetres 160–172cm equals 5ft 3in–5ft 8in and 146–162cm equals 4ft 9in–5ft 4in.

(Page 10)

Page 10 provides a summary of conclusions from the Activity on pages 8–9. Students should be encouraged to add more detail to their chart if necessary and to discuss why the skeletons do not provide answers to questions 3–5.

In **Source 4**, the top right-hand box can be linked to Isbister. Archaeologists think that the people of Isbister exposed the bodies of the dead before burying the remaining bones. It has also been suggested that this was a purpose of Stonehenge – a ceremonial site where bodies were left before the bones were buried elsewhere.

(Pages 11–12)
Can we learn about prehistoric medicine from people living today?

Pages 11–12 provide answers to questions 3–5 in the chart on page 8. Completing the chart can be the main focus for students' work. The Aborigines have been a staple of 'Medicine through Time' since the first materials were produced. Therefore, much of the same material has been repeated here for the sake of familiarity for many teachers, but it is also hoped that the value of this evidence is clearer because students will have realised from the chart activity that there are questions we cannot answer from archaeological evidence alone.

(Page 13)
Types of evidence

Activity: This gives students the chance to consolidate their knowledge of prehistoric medicine. If **Worksheet 7** is completed, students will show both basic knowledge of medicine and health, and an awareness of the evidence that supports these statements. Of the seven statements, only sentence 5 is clearly wrong. This could be corrected to refer to trephining (page 12). Other statements that could be amended are 4 (to include women as healers), 6 (to say that this was probably what they believed) and 7 (where skeletons tell us about health rather than medicine). For the most part, correct statements have been included to reduce the potential for confusion.

Question 1: More able students can be reminded that their answers are probably correct but we do not know for certain because of the absence of evidence.

Question 3: Worksheet 8 provides students with opening sentences to help them structure their answers.

Enquiry: Egypt, Greece and Rome: the great empires

Students' Book pp. 14–15
Worksheet 9, *also* 97 and 99

This spread has two objectives:

- to help students understand the chronology/sequence of the Egyptians, Greeks and Romans
- to start students thinking about whether medicine progressed in these empires. This revisits ideas from page 7.

Worksheet 9 is an unillustrated version of the timeline for students to complete.

Students find the chronology of these empires difficult to remember by the time they get to later periods, let alone their exam. The sequence is revisited several times in Chapter 6 but it will help if:

- a simple timeline is maintained on the classroom wall; and/or
- students regularly but briefly do sequencing exercises (using **Worksheets 97 and 99**). The pictures on these sheets need to be cut up and given, mixed up, to students for them to reorder correctly. This exercise is most effective when done for five minutes at frequent intervals rather than only once or twice during the course.

The other difficult chronological concept is prehistory which in terms of Britain overlaps the empires dealt with in the rest of this chapter. This is shown in the timeline and prehistory is explained in the cartoon at the top of page 14. The maps are to locate the empires but detailed work on the information boxes is not necessary.

Questions 1–4: These need only be tackled orally as they are intended to get students thinking about the main themes to come.

Question 1: Written evidence is the basic point here. It may be that students will have looked at different kinds of writing in KS2, e.g. hieroglyphs, or will know about the use of papyrus.

Question 2: Refer back to the Activity chart on page 8.

Questions 3 and 4 are deliberately not answered on these pages. Students should suggest 'yes' or 'no', perhaps using the information on the maps about the development of civilisations as evidence of new skills.

Enquiry: How did life in Egypt affect medicine?

Students' Book pp. 16–17
Worksheet 10

This spread introduces Egyptian society.

Activity: Worksheet 10 is to be used for the Activity on page 16. The main intention is to show that Egyptian medical developments were linked to changes in society rather than because the Egyptians were cleverer than people in prehistoric societies. These aspects of Egyptian society are examined in pages 17–19, especially the link between the Nile, irrigation and ideas about the causes of disease.

Enquiry: Who treated the sick in ancient Egypt?

Students' Book pp. 18–19
Worksheet 11

The spread provides evidence about the specialist doctors of Egypt and their skills. This needs to be contrasted with the idea that the specialist healers in prehistoric societies were 'medicine men'. Most of this material will be familiar from earlier versions of 'Medicine through Time' but **Source 5** on page 18 introduces the existence of a woman doctor.

Question 4 takes the issue of women's role in medicine further. Students could answer this by referring to assumptions that women were healers in prehistoric societies and that today they still attend to many everyday illnesses without the details finding their way into written records.

What did Egyptian healers know about the body and causes of disease?

Questions 5–6: There are two key ideas here:

- The link between embalming and knowledge of anatomy. Question 5 helps students to understand that embalming both helped and hindered the Egyptians' knowledge of the body. It is worth emphasising that anatomical knowledge was a by-product, not the main purpose, of embalming. Teachers keen to use brief role play could 'act out' the death of a Pharaoh, with a selected student lying flat on a large desk and the teacher acting as High Priest, explaining to the class of trainee priests what is about to happen to the Pharaoh's earthly body.

■ The link between Nile irrigation and explanations of the causes of disease. This has been briefly introduced on page 17. Diagrams on the board, showing irrigation channels and body channels, side by side, will help to get across the parallel. It is important to make the parallel explicit, and challenge the likely response that this explanation was simple or stupid. Students need to see this as a common-sense, logical explanation linked to the Egyptians' way of life. With some classes it may help if the teacher argues that the idea of blocked channels was foolish, thus challenging students to explain why it was logical.

Activity: Worksheet 11 provides a full-page copy of the chart on Egyptian medicine for students to complete.

Enquiry: How did the Egyptians treat illnesses and injuries?

Students' Book pp. 20–21

Question 1 is intended as a comprehension/organising exercise, i.e.:

■ herbs (Sources 2 and 4)
■ surgery (Source 3)
■ magic/charms (Source 5) (reference could also be made to scarabs used as charms)
■ others: prevention (Sources 1 and 6) and purging (Source 6)

   Source 5 foreshadows the Greek Asclepeia and may be returned to later.
   Source 7 does not fit into an obvious category. Today we would perhaps categorise it as superstition/magic but it may be that in past societies the use of mice was more akin to herbal treatments. Mice were also used in nineteenth-century remedies in Britain (see page 121, square 18).
   This spread also introduces themes that will be repeated a number of times throughout the course:
   Question 3 comments on the parallel use of practical effective cures and of 'magical' cures.
   Question 5 shows the effectiveness of herbal remedies.
   Question 7 has two elements to the answer:

■ the absence of scientifically proved cures
■ the likely fact that the use of mice did not do any observable harm.

Activity: it will help many students if they can look at contemporary advertisements for such items as toothpaste, headache tablets and cough mixtures. Although they will have seen these

many times they may not have paid much attention to the detail of wording/slogans or their claims to success.

Enquiry: Egyptian medicine: a summary

Students' Book pp. 22–23
Worksheets 12, 13

If students have completed Worksheet 11 as they have worked through pages 18–21, they will have their own summary of Egyptian medicine.
   Worksheet 12 will help students structure the essay set in the **Task** on page 22 by providing introductory sentences for each paragraph and ideas for material to include in the essay.
   Question 1 (linked to the cartoon) asks students to explain the reasons for changes in medicine. Pages 16–17 or students' annotated Worksheet 10 will be particularly helpful.

Were there medical developments in other places?

One of the temptations with the history of medicine is to be encyclopaedic, making reference to as many cultures as possible. However, leaping around the world adds an extra burden for students who are trying to cope with detail, chronology and understanding of, for example, Egyptian medicine. Therefore, this book deliberately does not range too far into Chinese, Indian or other medicines. Page 23 simply aims to show that the Egyptians were not the only people to develop medical skills. It is not trying to identify particular developments with specific societies. Therefore, the **Activity** of completing the map on **Worksheet 13** should suffice to show the range of societies that were developing new medical methods. Of course this does not stop teachers using their own knowledge and enthusiasm to explore any of these other early cultures. Such enthusiasm is usually a good route to a memorable lesson.

Enquiry: Greek medicine: what happened at an Asclepion?

Students' Book pp. 24–25

Work on Greek medicine begins with a continuity – the importance of religion in medicine and healing. Starting with continuities is likely to be more effective than first plunging into new ideas and then going back to continuities. Students need to see the Greek

Asclepeia in a similar light to prehistoric and Egyptian beliefs in spirits and also as a development in the building of sophisticated temples. Reference to page 20, Source 5 shows the overlap between Egyptian and Greek ideas.

Source 1, Question 1: Note the continuing role of women in medicine.

Source 2, Question 3: The emphasis on fitness, etc., shows that there was a rational side to the use of Asclepeia. Students should see from this that residence at the temple might well help some people recover. This could be built into the **Activity** with some students suffering from headaches, tiredness (or other signs of exam stress!!) as well as the more serious problems described in **Sources 3 and 4**.

Enquiry: Why did the Greeks have new ideas about medicine?

Students' Book pp. 26–28

After the enjoyment of the snakes and miracles of the Asclepeia comes the difficult theory of the four humours. This is a key idea because of its long-lasting effect on the history of medicine, which was felt well into the nineteenth century. There are two stages here:

The theory of the four humours

Stage i: at this first stage, students need to understand the theory that the body contains four humours and that people become ill when the humours get out of balance. One method of explanation would be for the teacher to play the role of Hippocrates instructing his students. Begin by saying how and why the Egyptians were wrong about the causes of disease and then explain your own theory using **Source 1**. In your role as Hippocrates ask questions such as 'Do you know what humours are?' 'What happens if you have a cold in winter?' After you have explained the theory, ask recap, factual questions – 'Tell me two of the four humours', 'What are the other two?' etc.

Why did the Greeks develop the theory of the four humours?

Stage ii: as with the Egyptians, students need to understand that the Greek belief in the four humours did not materialise out of thin air. It will make more sense if they realise that:

- Greek society was wealthy, giving time for study.
- The theory was based on careful observation of the body's behaviour during illness. Symptoms such as vomiting, sweating and

diarrhoea were interpreted as evidence of the humours being out of balance.

Sources 2–5 show the links between the theory of the four humours and other Greek explanations of the world around them.

Activity: Sources 2–5 can be used as the basis for the Activity. Questions can range from 'What are the four humours?' to 'Which humour do you have too much of if you have a nose bleed/sneezing?' and 'At which time of year do people have too much phlegm?'

Enquiry: Who treated the sick in ancient Greece?

Students' Book p. 29
Worksheet 14

Task: Despite the emphasis on doctors and humours, students also need to recognise the continuities in medicine. By completing the chart it will be clear that there was the same range of healers. Reference back to the Asclepius is needed (see pages 24–25).

Source 1: The various threads of Hippocrates' contribution are drawn together on pages 32–33.

Source 2: Note the reference to Asclepius.

Source 3: Worksheet 14 contains questions that the city's rulers might have put to Hagnodice after she had been discovered working as a doctor. Students could work individually or in pairs to devise Hagnodice's answers.

Enquiry: How did Greek doctors prevent and treat illnesses?

Students' Book pp. 30–31

This spread underlines the logical, scientific approach of some Greek doctors, linking medical methods to the theory of the four humours.

Treatments

Source 2: Note continued use of herbs within an approach based on the four humours.

Question 5 is for students to think about rather than seeking the answer in text and sources. The advice in **Sources 4 and 5** suggests wealth and time which ordinary Greeks simply did not have.

Developments on these pages can be noted in students' factors grids under Science and Technology, and under War.

Enquiry: Hippocrates – the greatest doctor of them all?

Students' Book pp. 32–33

This is very much a summary spread, recapping the different elements of the work and ideas associated with Hippocrates. Entries can be made in students' factors grids under Individuals and Communications.

Question 3 needs a general rather than a specific answer. Reference can be made to the lack of scientific knowledge and equipment, such as microscopes, and that the existing explanation seemed logical and consistent to the Greeks. Why should they seek another?

This spread provides another opportunity for role play with one student in every group of three or four playing the part of Hippocrates and answering questions for interviewers on his achievements. This would be particularly helpful with Question 3 when Hippocrates could make it clear that he believed he already knew the true causes of illness and so had no need to look for other explanations that we now know to be correct.

Enquiry: Greek and Egyptian medicine: a summary comparison

Students' Book p. 34

This page looks at the similarities and differences between the two civilisations. Students not only need to identify these similarities and differences, but also to understand the reasons for continuities and changes. Teachers could work through the chart at the top of the page, asking the class or groups to explain why, for example, both Egyptians and Greeks had priests as healers or why the Greeks bled the sick and the Egyptians did not.

Task 1, Question 1: Hopefully students will choose (d) but they might also choose (c) because this would contribute to (d). Verbally students might explain why they have not chosen the other three possibilities.

Task 1, Question 3: Hippocrates might have opted for (a) or (b). He would not have chosen (d) because he believed he already knew the causes of disease and may not have seen the need for (c).

Task 2, Question 2: A more structured version of this question would be to give students subheadings and ask them to write captions explaining how each factor held up

progress. Subheadings could be religion, technology, limited knowledge of the body, conservatism (referring to the belief that they already understood the causes of disease).

Source 1 can be used to add material to students' factors grids.

Enquiry: Why was Alexandria so important?

Students' Book p. 35

This page demonstrates aspects of Greek medicine other than the work of Hippocrates:

- new ideas about the working of the body, particularly the role of the brain
- the importance of Alexandria as a centre of knowledge.

The text mentions that Erasistratus did not believe in the theory of the four humours. Students might be asked why others did not agree with Erasistratus and whether the impact of Hippocrates was negative, i.e. did it stop others enquiring into the causes of disease?

Enquiry: Was the Roman Empire different from the Greek Empire?

Students' Book p. 36

This page creates the transition into Roman medicine. It will be useful to refer back to the timeline and maps on pages 14–15. The main theme of the chapter (see page 40) will be whether Roman medicine was the same as Greek medicine. Students are asked to suggest an early answer to that question.

Sources 1 and 2 can be used as a quarry for ideas. Source 1 suggests the continuities between the two societies but ideas about differences can be found in Source 2.

Enquiry: A Roman army hospital

Students' Book pp. 37–39
Worksheet 15

A change of pace and variety is provided by the extract from the novel *The Silver Pigs* by Lindsey Davis. This extract can be found on pages 111–113 of the Pan paperback first published in 1989 and still available. This is the first of a series of novels all featuring the same hero and all great fun as well as evoking Roman life.

Activity: The main purpose of the Activity on page 37 is to gain a sense of Roman surgical methods, from the story itself and then from **Sources 2–8** on pages 38–39.

Worksheet 15 is a copy of the extract which students should use for the Activity. Reference should be made to the sources, e.g. **Source 7** provides evidence for the hot turnip mash mentioned at the end of the extract.

An example of Romano-British medicine can be found in *The Eagle of the Ninth* by Rosemary Sutcliffe. Pages 184–185 of the Puffin edition describe the use of toad-fat and salves to cure a child's sore eyes; this contrasts different approaches to medicine.

Enquiry: Were Roman medical ideas the same as those of the Greeks?

Students' Book pp. 40–42
Worksheet 16

Activity: Worksheet 16 provides the thread that pulls together the material on Roman medicine. Students can keep adding material up to and including page 47. The basic pattern is of continuity with the addition of a new emphasis on public health.

The text on pages 40–42 provides basic material for completing Worksheet 16. This can be tackled by each student simply working through the text and questions. Alternatively, students could work in small groups – playing the part of Greek doctors arriving in Rome to see what, if anything, they can learn – or perhaps of Greek medical inspectors checking the effectiveness of Roman medicine. Working to an inspection report, students could use the material on pages 40–42 as evidence for their reports or quiz the teacher in the role of a Roman doctor about his/her methods and ideas.

Enquiry: What made Galen famous?

Students' Book pp. 43–45
Worksheet 17

These pages provide a summary of Galen's work, paralleling it with that of Hippocrates. Galen's role is important to establish because his work dominated medical theories for the next 1000 years.

Students may be helped to enjoy this topic by using the **Activity** on page 45 as a starting point rather than as an 'after the event' piece of work.

The topic could be set up by announcing that the Emperor needs a new doctor and that anyone well qualified can apply. Students might then be asked to suggest, using the previous work on Roman medicine, what would count as well qualified:

■ training?
■ belief in the four humours?
■ experience?

Students, individually or in pairs, could take on the role of Galen, completing the job application/CV on **Worksheet 17** from the material on pages 43–45. If possible, a word-processed application could be completed. Once the applications are finished the teacher as the Emperor could interview the class as Galen, thereby going over their grasp of the material. Finally, more formal notes and written work could complete the topic. One element that may help to bring the topic to life is Galen's willingness to criticise others, his lack of tact and diplomacy – students could be encouraged to bring the tone of 'I am the best' into the final section of the CV on why Galen would be good at the job.

Galen's work could be entered on factor grids.

Enquiry: What was the Romans' big idea?

Students' Book pp. 46–47
Worksheets 18, 19

The best starting point for this topic may be the **Activity** on page 47 with students working in groups of three as different people in the Roman Empire. Alternatively, individuals or pairs could take on a role and report back their conclusion to the teacher in a whole-class session. If this Activity is done first then the answers, after discussion with the whole class, will help students to tackle the questions on page 47 and the **Activity** on page 46 more fully.

Source 5 gives some specific detail for the soldier in Wroxeter but students will also need to generalise from the rest of the information on the page. If they need structured help, **Worksheet 18** provides headings and questions.

After this work, entries can be made on the factors grids for Governments and Communications.

Task: Worksheet 19 provides a paragraph structure for this essay with introductory sentences and suggestions for detail. Students who have fully completed the chart on page 40 (Worksheet 16) will have ready-made material for the essay.

Enquiry: So ... did the Romans have new ideas?

Students' Book p. 48
Worksheet 20

Task: Worksheet 20 can be used as a revision exercise as well as part of the main body of work.

Question 1: On Worksheet 20 students need to identify each of the four pictures as reflecting either change or continuity.

Question 2: Students should add examples to their factors grids to show how each of the factors influenced change or continuity. This could be done as an individual or class activity and would then enable students to add any missing items to their factors grids.

Enquiry: Change and continuity in Roman Britain

Students' Book p. 49
Worksheet 21

This page links back to the earlier work on prehistoric Britain, looking at the impact of the Roman Empire. It tries to show that the impact of the Romans was not uniform but varied considerably according to the wealth and status of individuals. **Worksheet 21** provides extra source material about health in Roman Britain with an **Activity** to complete.

Enquiry: Would you survive in ancient Rome?

Students' Book pp. 50–51
Worksheets 22, 23

Worksheet 22 provides a photocopiable version of the gameboard. Students can complete **Worksheet 23** as they play – or at the second time of playing. With this kind of activity, it is often helpful for students just to play the game first time round and then play again, choosing a different character or symptom, and this time noting down the decisions they took and what happened to them.

The game has a variety of purposes – a change of activity will help to keep interest going; it can also help students' knowledge of treatments and

healers available. It is more likely that the patients will die rather than recover! It would also be possible to use this as an introduction to rather than a conclusion of Roman medicine.

After the organised fun of playing the game the debriefing is important, to compare the experiences of the patients. Was one family more likely to survive? Was one healer more effective? What different kinds of treatment could you get for the same symptoms?

Enquiry: From prehistory to the Romans: how much change?

Students' Book pp. 52–54
Worksheets 24, 25, 26, 27

These pages summarise the main themes from prehistory to Roman medicine.

Worksheet 24: Students can complete their version of the chart on page 52 so that they think about the content rather than simply gazing at the completed chart. The important details in the chart provide evidence to support statements a–c in **Question 3** of the **Task** on page 52. One way to approach this is to write each of the statements on the board as headings and ask students to add information from the chart under each heading as evidence. The balance of evidence would then suggest which statement was most accurate. It will probably be b!

Worksheets 25 and 26 provide structured guidance for the essays in **Task 2**, page 53.

(Page 54)
The health jigsaw AD200

This jigsaw is the first of four jigsaw illustrations. Their intention is to show how doctors were struggling to solve the problems of disease but could not do so until the right piece of the jigsaw – germ theory – had been discovered.

The best use of this picture may come after work has been completed on the Middle Ages, when students can compare the jigsaws for AD200 and AD1400 and look for similarities and differences.

Activity: Further information on Hippocrates and Galen can be found on **Worksheet 27**. If half the class tackles Hippocrates and the other half studies Galen it could lead into a debate/discussion of which was the more influential figure and whether either did a great deal actually to help their patients.

Chapter 2: Medicine and health AD 500–1400

Students' Book p. 55

Did medicine grow worse in the Middle Ages?

The beginning of this chapter (pages 55–61) identifies the main pattern of medicine in the Middle Ages. At its simplest, page 55 offers students three possible patterns of medical development which are shown in the graphs. All that needs to be done here is for students to predict what they think the pattern will turn out to be – will it be graph A, B or C. Predictions can be based on their KS3 work on the Middle Ages through comparing Roman and medieval homes/castles. This is not about getting the right answer straightaway but about thinking and predicting. The names of students choosing each of the three graphs could be listed on the wall or board before looking at pages 56–57.

Enquiry: Why were they still reading Galen in 1400?

Students' Book pp. 56–57

This spread identifies the pattern for the Middle Ages as being graph C on page 55. This is obviously a simplification and at the end of the chapter (pages 78–79) it is made clear that the patterns would have been different for rich and poor. However, for the moment, the simplicity of one pattern is sufficient.

If students did choose one graph from page 55, the first task here is to ask 'who got it right'? Use the material to decide which graph is the most accurate. This will help students establish an outline pattern in their minds and in their books. The **Task** will similarly start them thinking about the factors that affected medicine. Notes could be added to students' factors grids.

Enquiry: Did health decline in the Middle Ages? A case study of York

Students' Book pp. 58–61
Worksheet 28

This four-page unit focuses on the patterns of individual and public health rather than that of medical knowledge. The pattern of public health that emerges is similar to that in the previous summary spread – disintegration and regression followed by continuity and then recovery.

(Pages 58–59)
The **Task** on page 58 will help students to record information in note form and will help them with their chronology. The sense of difference within the Middle Ages may be achieved by asking groups of students to report on health and public health in each of the four periods (Roman, Saxon, Viking and Norman York) – perhaps on the evidence if they time-travelled back to the past. Details of the impact of war, etc., can be entered on timelines and students' factors grids.

(Pages 60–61)
Worksheet 28 provides an essay structure for the **Task** on page 61. Opening sentences are given for each paragraph to help students to structure written work.

Enquiry: The Black Death: a case study in medieval medicine

Students' Book pp. 62–65
Worksheet 29

The Black Death is a topic students may well remember from Year 7 work because of the gruesome details! The emphasis here is on what medieval reactions to the pestilence tell us about their ideas on the causes of disease. However, the events themselves provide a good opportunity for some riveting storytelling, especially if the teacher takes on the role of a survivor: telling of the first rumours; then the symptoms (a squash ball under the armpit makes a very convincing swelling, especially if dropped at a strategic moment in the story) and finally of fright.

(Pages 62–63)
This material provides the basis for such storytelling. An excellent source of contemporary material can be found in Dr Rosemary Horrox (ed.) *The Black Death* (Manchester University Press, 1994). This includes accounts of the spread of the pestilence, its effects and explanations of what caused the outbreak.

(Pages 64–65)
What did they think caused the Black Death?

Activity: Worksheet 29 provides the basis for work on what people saw as the causes of the Black Death. The extracts on these pages show a wide variety of explanations, although if they accurately reflected contemporary ideas a high proportion would echo the belief in **Source 9** that the disease was a punishment from God.

Unfortunately, there simply isn't space to reflect that balance or to quote extracts in full. Dr Horrox's book contains the accounts in full.

The teaching problem is to get beyond the reaction of 'weren't they stupid to believe that?' What needs to be emphasised is that there are some common-sense, intelligent reactions here (see also Source 7, page 63) despite the absence of the scientific equipment that later allowed the discovery of germs.

Source 8 can be compared with earlier Roman ideas about invisible carriers of disease to show that intelligent observation was not new in the nineteenth century. This can be reinforced by the next spread on fourteenth-century London.

Enquiry: What did they do about public health in fourteenth-century London?

Students' Book pp. 66–67
Worksheets 30, 31

The answer is often assumed to be 'nothing', that medieval people were entirely careless of public health. However, contemporary evidence, some of which is reflected here and on **Worksheet 31**, suggests that there was concern about living conditions even if it was more difficult to take effective action. Most of the evidence can be interpreted in two different ways, for example – do we deduce that people were careless about health because they threw their rubbish into the streets or do we put more emphasis on the fact that they could be arrested and fined for doing so?

Worksheet 30 provides a 'Where's Wally?' exercise. Students should find the 14 points on page 67 in the picture and mark/annotate them on the worksheet. The purpose of this type of exercise is to make students focus on the detail before answering the more general questions. A good description of London at this time can be found in Barbara Hanawalt, *Growing up in Medieval London* (OUP, 1993). In the paperback the relevant pages are 22–39. Richard Whittington, Lord Mayor, left money to build one of London's public latrines – it had 64 seats for men and 64 for women.

Enquiry: What did a doctor need to know in the Middle Ages?

Students' Book pp. 68–71

The Middle Ages is often seen as a period of complete regression. Medieval doctors are regarded as less effective than Hippocrates and Galen even though they followed the same ideas and methods, and developed skills of their own based on practical experience. These pages try to show the skills as well as the limitations of the medieval doctor.

(Pages 68–69)
How were doctors trained?
Activity: This could be the basis for the production of posters for rival medical schools, each representing a group of students. (The **Activity** on page 71 returns to this prospectus.) If schools have DTP facilities it is a good opportunity to use that technology.

Two recent books that contain much more material on medieval medicine are M.L. Cameron, *Anglo-Saxon Medicine* (CUP) and C. Rawcliffe, *Medicine in Later Medieval England* (Alan Sutton Publishing).

Task: For ease of reference the answers are:

a) False; women could only become surgeons
b) True
c) False
d) False
e) True.

Enquiry: Did medieval hospitals help the sick?

Students' Book pp. 72–73
Worksheet 32

This spread continues to look at the two sides of medieval medicine – practical attempts to cure illness alongside an inability to tackle many health problems. There are two sets of similarities and differences here:

- between hospitals then and now
- between hospitals in Europe and in the Islamic world.

Activity: Worksheet 32 contains a copy of **Source 2**. Students can mark on this many of the features described on page 73.

Entries can be made on the factors grid for Religion and, perhaps, for Individuals – Richard Whittington.

Enquiry: Was Arab medicine more advanced than European medicine?

Students' Book pp. 74–75

Although the main theme, for the sake of directness and simplicity, is European medicine, a contrast with Arab medicine is important.

Source 2 on page 68 has already shown that Guy de Chauliac read the work of leading Arab doctors. **Source 1** on page 74 is intended to contrast the approaches of east and west through vivid stories. The Arab methods are seen as more logical and effective in the first case but the second story shows a successful, practical cure by the Franks.

Enquiry: Did the Christian Church help or hinder medical progress?

Students' Book pp. 76–77

Religion and the role of the Church has necessarily been an important theme in this chapter. This spread uses the **Task** on page 76 to pull together the threads of this theme. The Task sets up a research exercise that could be undertaken by individual students or broken up amongst a class and the results recorded on the board. After this exercise has been completed, students can enter summary conclusions under Religion on their factors grid.

Enquiry: Did health and medicine grow worse in the Middle Ages?

Students' Book pp. 78–79

This spread summarises changes in medical care and its effects on health. The graphs return to the introductory page of the chapter but show that there were different problems for different classes. This reflects the theme at the end of Chapter 1 – that the impact of Roman medicine on ordinary people was very limited. Throughout the Middle Ages they continued to use herbal remedies and other ancient treatments, unheeding of the words of Galen and Avicenna, etc. One way to emphasise this would be to divide the class – two-thirds as the poor (page 78), one-third as the wealthy (page 79) – and have each group report on changes to their families' health and medical experience during the Middle Ages.

Enquiry: Was there more continuity than change in the Middle Ages?

Students' Book pp. 80–82
Worksheet 33

These pages summarise the main themes of Chapter 2, building on the summary chart at the end of Chapter 1.

Worksheet 33 provides a copy of the summary chart for students to complete. (The worksheet could be enlarged to A3 size.) These overview issues will be returned to in Chapter 6 but that work will be based on more solid ground if conclusions have been drawn at this stage.

(Page 82)
The health jigsaw AD1400

The jigsaw summarises changes and continuities during the Middle Ages.

Chapter 3: Medicine and health AD1400–1750

This chapter contains a good deal of material that will be familiar to anyone who has been teaching 'medicine'. The old favourites – Vesalius, Paré and Harvey – are here but new material has been added to investigate how their discoveries affected medical practice.

Enquiry: Did the Medical Renaissance improve people's health?

Students' Book p. 83

This introductory page repeats the predicting exercise from Chapter 2. This raises the central conceptual problem of the period – that improvements in medical knowledge did not lead to immediate improvements in treatments and health, except in the limited area of some surgical treatments. The **Task**, asking students to choose the graph that they think will prove correct, is intended to raise the possibility in students' minds that improvement in medical knowledge did not automatically equal improvements in health. Therefore this page needs brief but clear coverage – again a list could be made of who chose which graph and this can be returned to at the end of the chapter.

Enquiry: How did Vesalius change the way the human body was studied?

Students' Book pp. 84–85

This spread presents Vesalius' work on two levels – the key points in the box on page 84 and then in a more detailed form in the text. The interview format may help students to pick out the key details because of the way the questions are posed.

Activity: One approach is to divide the tasks between the class; one half criticising Vesalius and the other half praising him. An additional oral question that needs to be asked at the end of this spread is whether students think Vesalius' work would have affected health and treatments.

Enquiry: Why did Paré make new surgical discoveries?

Students' Book pp. 86–87
Worksheet 34

The text on these pages tries to tell Paré's story in an interesting style but more entertaining would be a piece of storytelling by the teacher in the role of Paré, explaining how he ran out of oil and then tried an alternative treatment. This needs to be separated from Problem 2. In such a role-play Paré should be puzzled as to why his ligatures did not save more lives. If students enjoyed the interview format of the Vesalius pages, they could suggest questions they would ask Paré in an interview.

At the end of this unit, students could be asked orally whether Paré's discoveries had a greater impact on health and treatments than did Vesalius' discoveries. This might then be related to the introductory graphs on page 83. However, the point need not be laboured at this stage.

Worksheet 34 provides additional material on Paré with some questions to answer.

Enquiry: What was William Harvey's great discovery?

Students' Book pp. 88–89

A set of comprehension questions will help students to glean the basic points from this spread:

1. What did doctors think about the blood before Harvey's work?
2. What did Harvey say about how the blood moves around the body?
3. How did Harvey prove his theory about the circulation of the blood?
4. Why did some doctors think Harvey was wrong?

Enquiry: What caused these discoveries?

Students' Book pp. 90–91
Worksheet 35

The spreads on Vesalius, Paré and Harvey all looked at the reasons for their discoveries. This spread pulls those themes together to gain an overview of the reasons for the Medical Renaissance.

Activity: Worksheet 35 provides a copy of the chart on page 90 for duplication. Students can either tackle the Activity for each of the three individuals or different groups could work on individuals.

Alternatively, teachers may build up the connections using a chart on the board with the whole class, asking for each of the connections to be explained. Although the topic is presented here as one spread, it needs as much time spent on it as the next ten pages together.

Enquiry: Did the Medical Renaissance improve health and treatments?

Students' Book pp. 92–101
Worksheet 36

The impact of the discoveries of Vesalius, Paré and Harvey is first assessed through the four case studies in this section.

Activity: It will not be necessary for students to cover all the case studies on pages 92–101. The topics could be divided within the class with each student studying one or two topics and then the overall conclusions collated on **Worksheet 36** (a copy of the chart). The main themes are as follows:

Grace Mildmay:	■ knowledge of works of Galen, Avicenna and others
	■ use of bleeding and herbal remedies
	■ use of new ideas of Paracelsus.
Richard Wiseman:	■ knowledge of Paré's work but use of oil
	■ use of herbal remedies learned from observation and experience
	■ apparent belief in royal touch.
The Great Plague 1665:	■ inability of doctors to cure disease
	■ intelligent measures to stop spread of plague
	■ use of charms and illogical cures.
James Woodforde:	■ use of herbal remedies and bleeding
	■ use of inoculation against smallpox
	■ attitude to use of cat's tail as a cure.

The case studies show there was great continuity, with the work of Galen and medieval doctors still being followed, but there were some signs of change too. It is this overall pattern which students need to understand rather than having detailed knowledge of all the case studies.

(Page 96)
Activity: Here are some sample questions, in case students need help.

1. How did you learn to be a surgeon?
2. Have you read the books of any ancient doctors?
3. Do you agree with their ideas?
4. Do you follow Paré's methods?
5. Do you use herbal remedies?
6. How do you treat wounds?
7. Why did you write your books about surgery?

(Page 97)
The Great Plague: 1665

Activity: For ease of reference the answers are as follows.

Explanations	Treatments
Conjunction of comets	prayers and fasting
God's anger	avoiding contact
Spread by contact/breath	wearing charms
Carried in the air by invisible creatures	use of chickens or pigeons on sores

In essence, both explanations and treatments are very similar to those of the fourteenth century.

(Pages 100–101)
James Woodforde, parson and diarist (1740–1803)

Questions 1–6: For ease of reference the answers are as follows.

1. Rhubarb. The root of the plant is shown in **Source 19**.
2. Inoculation against smallpox, emetics for causing vomiting, herbs, quinine for fever, cold water for stye on his eyelid.
3. Measles, smallpox.
4. Inoculation.
5. His doctor's treatment – in the end!
6. More similarities with Galen although some treatments would be used today.

Activity: This could form a significant class database if students take it seriously and could be used to support the Activity on page 159.

Enquiry: Great medical discoveries! No one healthier!

Students' Book pp. 102–103
Worksheet 37

This spread summarises the impact of the Medical Renaissance.

Task: Source 1 shows that life expectancy was not increasing. **Source 2** lists the most common causes of death but also suggests the vagueness of medical detail. It should be noted that Source 1 includes infant deaths (i.e. all those under the age of 20) but Source 10 on page 61 does not.

(Page 103)
The health jigsaw 1700

The health jigsaw, compared with similar earlier pictures, should emphasise the continuities.

Question 2: Worksheet 37 provides an essay structure to help answer the question.

Enquiry: Who would you go to for treatment?

Students' Book p. 104

This page also emphasises continuity in that there were many healers who were qualified through experience rather than academic study.

Activity: Individual students could take on one of the roles a–d listed in the Activity, and then report back to the class on who they would consult when ill, and why. This exercise could be repeated with different kinds of symptoms – varying in seriousness – to show that there was a range of healers offering a variety of treatments.

Enquiry: How did the status of women healers change?

Students' Book p. 105

One of the themes in each section has been the role of women in healing. Again, the emphasis is on continuity and change in this period, with women being excluded from the treatment of wealthier patients. Reference could be made back to Lady Grace Mildmay's attitude that women should not be involved in surgery (page 92). One route to understanding this issue would be to set up a debate between women surgeons and male doctors or for students to write a letter justifying the exclusion of women from surgery.

Enquiry: How would you treat Charles II?

Students' Book pp. 106–107 and p. 110
Worksheet 38

Activity: The death of Charles II has long been a favourite topic – this game approaches it from a different angle. It brings together the continued reliance on bleeding and purges, etc., and the use of some (to us) very eccentric cures combined with hostility to capable women healers. The game is meant to be fun and may be best organised with students working in pairs, competing to see which pair scores the most points. Nevertheless, students should reach some understanding of how similar medicine was in 1685 to that of 1500 years earlier.

Enquiry: Medicine from prehistory to 1750: a summary

Students' Book pp. 108–109
Worksheets 39, 40

Continuing the format of earlier summaries, these pages compare developments in the period 1400–1750 with earlier periods.

Task 1: Worksheet 39 – students can complete the final column of the chart to summarise their work on this chapter. (The worksheet could be enlarged to A3 size.)

Task 2 offers a list of topics for discussion – these could be used to underline the key themes although you may feel that some of them have already been covered sufficiently.

Task 3 can be used to add further detail to students' factors grids.

Task 4: Worksheet 40 provides help with structuring the essay.

Chapter 4: Medicine and health 1750–1900

Why was there so much progress in this period?

This chapter looks at the period in which, it is often claimed, there were great advances in medicine. Three main areas will be investigated:

■ scientists and doctors made giant steps forward in the understanding of the causes of disease
■ they discovered ways of preventing some of the killer diseases
■ there were enormous improvements in public health.

This is a period with which the students may have some familiarity through their study of Britain 1750–1900. The opening cartoon on page 111 prompts a discussion about how much medicine and health improved for ordinary people from 1750 to 1900. In this chapter students can decide if the news vendor is right.

Enquiry: Why had they stopped reading Galen in the nineteenth century?

Students' Book p. 112

This page summarises how far Galen's ideas had been gradually superseded by theories formed as a result of new scientific methods and technologies, especially the development of microscopes. There are also aspects of continuity in that there was still no scientific explanation for disease until the middle of the nineteenth century. This is a point that needs to be emphasised.

Source 1 requires students to apply their existing knowledge about Galen to the changing nineteenth-century view of the world with new scientific and rational knowledge.

Enquiry: How did changes in the nineteenth century affect medicine and health?

Students' Book p. 113
Worksheet 41

Pages 112–113 together cover some very complex changes, albeit changes which students will be familiar with from their earlier study of history. The **Task** on page 113 covers both pages and is designed simply to stimulate discussion of both **Sources 1 and 3**. Page 113 summarises the key features of the nineteenth century.

Worksheet 41 can be used to record comments and information as they emerge. The worksheet also provides a useful reference point for work that follows later in this chapter and in Chapter 6.

Enquiry: What did people die of in the nineteenth century?

Students' Book pp. 114–115
Worksheets 42, 43, 44

As an introduction to the nineteenth century you could use **Worksheet 42** which describes Queen Victoria's sewage problems. Don't tell the students it is the Royal Family until after they have analysed the source. Then you could make the link: if this was the Royal Family's experience then what would conditions be like for the poorest?

The statistics in this section are intended to provide a picture of the health of people in one community. Most students will be able to cope better with these figures than with the thousands and millions that are often used to describe the national scene. The table in **Source 2** is complex and will need some explanation. This may be an opportunity to use IT if time can be invested in entering the statistics into a spreadsheet. Local examples of this sort of table are commonly available for nearly every community in the country. Ask at your local record office for the Medical Officer of Health's Annual Reports.

Task: The questions should draw out fundamental information: that, unlike today, infectious disease was a great killer; that children under the age of five were the most vulnerable group in society and that many diseases which we can cure today could not be cured even at the end of the nineteenth century.

The top four killers for under fives were: bronchitis, measles, diphtheria and diarrhoea.

For over fives they were: bronchitis, heart disease, phthisis (TB) and diphtheria.

Worksheet 43 is intended as a means of recording information and comparing it with modern statistics (see page 170).

Activity: Worksheet 44 is a template for students to complete for the Activity on page 115.

Enquiry: Smallpox: how did Jenner make his breakthrough?

Students' Book pp. 116–118
Worksheets 45, 46

Arguably the greatest medical triumph of the eighteenth and nineteenth centuries was the prevention of smallpox. Jenner succeeded in developing further the techniques of inoculation brought to this country from Turkey. His conscientous observations and his luck in encountering cowpox were exploited to the full. The result was that the worst impact of the most deadly disease of the period was to a great extent averted. Again, an example from a locality has been chosen to illustrate the scale of deaths. (Question 1 (page 117) in the first printing of this book wrongly referred students to Source 3 on page 116. It should be Source 2 on page 114. This was corrected in later printings.) By using Maidstone again it is possible to refer to the Medical Officer of Health's Report of 1889 and make further comparisons. There is clear statistical evidence that the incidence of smallpox in the town declined once Daniel Sutton began mass inoculations.

On page 117 the issue of compulsion is worth exploring in discussion, with reference to recent vaccination campaigns, especially for babies. Should parents be allowed free choice?

(Pages 118–119)
Why was there opposition to vaccination?

Questions 1 and 2 compare two different views of the work of Jenner. The cartoons are by two of the greatest cartoonists of the day. **Worksheet 45** provides students with their own copies of the cartoons to annotate.

(Page 119)
How important was Jenner's work?

Activity: Worksheet 46 is a template for the encyclopaedia entry about Jenner which acts as a summary Activity for this enquiry with the emphasis on the role of the individual.

As a starter for this Activity you could discuss in class the reasons why the sculptor has shown eight-year-old James Phipps as a toddler.

Enquiry: Would your child survive in nineteenth-century Britain?

Students' Book pp. 120–121
Worksheets 47, 48

Activity: This game is designed to draw students into the period, to place them in the same position as people at the time. It is impossible to reconstruct the past with all its complexities but this game requires students to make decisions for reasons that would have been valid at the time. The disease in the game is whooping cough but students don't need to know that in advance. By photocopying the game on **Worksheet 48** and increasing it to A3, students will find it easier to read and more manageable.

After completing the Activity, debate the accuracy of such an exercise and discuss why it is useful in a textbook at this level.

Question 7: Worksheet 47 is provided to help students record the information they collect.

Enquiry: Were doctors and medicine helpful?

Students' Book pp. 122–123

Not many had access to doctors in the early nineteenth century, but since doctors could cure very few diseases at that time perhaps this did not matter to people.

Sources 1 and 2: The study of patent medicines is fascinating. Adverts for these can be found in any local newspaper of the time. People bought patent medicines as a cheap alternative to medical care in the hope that they would work. Many were addictive and some were poisonous. The government made so much money from the duty on these products that they were very slow to enforce standards on the manufacturers.

It is always helpful if you can find information about local doctors to illustrate their work in the area. The best book for teachers on this topic is by Irvine Loudon.

The **Activity** on continuity and change helps bring together a clear statement about the main features of medicine and health during the period 1700–1900.

Enquiry: Could you see a woman doctor in the 1850s?

Students' Book pp. 124–125
Worksheets 49, 50, 51

The recognition of women doctors was a hard-fought battle. It was also one which led the way in dismantling some of the limitations on the role of middle-class women in the nineteenth century. See also *The Changing Role of Women* by Liz Bellamy and Kate Moorse (in the Discovering the Past series) which fills in the background to this enquiry and shows the part the struggle for recognition in medicine played in the wider fight for women's rights.

Activity: Worksheet 49 can be cut up to provide cards for students to match.

Question 5: Worksheet 50 helps students to explain how each of the factors listed helped to limit or increase the role of women in medicine.

Nursing

Task: Worksheet 51 on Mary Seacole provides sources from her autobiography which identify her training, her methods of treatment and the impact she had on those around her. While not central to many medicine syllabuses, Mary Seacole is an ideal contrast and counterpoint to Florence Nightingale.

Enquiry: How did Florence Nightingale improve hospitals?

Students' Book pp. 126–127

Activity: The story of Florence Nightingale in the Crimea is well known. Her years as the world authority on hospital design and nursing practice is often given a back seat. It was this aspect of her work which had the greatest impact on the health of ordinary people. See Dingwall, Rafferty and Webster, *An Introduction to the Social History of Nursing* (1988).

Enquiry: How did scientists discover the causes of disease?

Students' Book pp. 128–133
Worksheets 52, 53, 54, 55, 56, 57, 58, 59

Pasteur's germ theory was the great turning point in the period 1750–1900. Its impact cannot be underestimated for the century that followed. Remind students of their factors grids at the back of their books. The factors come thick and fast in this enquiry. They will also be helpful for the **Task** on page 133.

Steps 3 and 4: The science of this period is vital, for without these fundamental discoveries the developments in diagnosis, therapy and surgery could not have progressed at the pace they did in the late nineteenth and the twentieth centuries.

(Pages 128–129)
How did people explain disease in the 1800s?

Describing the miasma and spontaneous generation theories is complicated without simple graphical illustrations. These have been provided both in the textbook and on **Worksheet 52**.

Germ theory needs to be clearly understood because it is the basis of all subsequent developments.

Ask the science department if you can borrow a microscope and some appropriate slides. It is an interesting experience for students to be able to see exactly what the nineteenth-century scientists saw.

Task: Question 3: Taking a step-by-step approach to the discovery of the causes of disease is both logical and structured. A timeline might also help to set events in context.

Worksheet 53 is a flow chart which students can use.

(Page 130)
How important was Robert Koch?

Worksheet 54 is a cartoon of Robert Koch from **Source 3**. Annotating the cartoon on the worksheet simply provides an alternative approach to note taking.

Question 1: Worksheet 55 is a framework that provides a template for the completion of the interview with Robert Koch.

(Pages 131–133)
Did germ theory help scientists?

Page 133 introduces a note of caution in this section. You are unlikely to find a cure without understanding the cause (smallpox vaccination was an exception that proved the rule) so understanding causes is of course a step forward. However, it does not guarantee that you will find a cure. Students must be aware of the difference between the discovery and identification of what causes a disease and the ability to provide cures.

In the **Task** at the end of the section students are asked to explain the reasons for the success of these scientists.

Worksheet 56 is a copy of the chart to use for **Question 1**. When students have completed their chart it can be used to help them with the essay in **Question 2** 'Why were the causes of disease finally discovered in the 1860s and 1870s?'

Worksheet 57 provides alternative help for Question 2 with a framework for the essay.

Source 8: Worksheet 58 is an extension exercise which ensures students have understood the key developments described in Source 8.

Worksheet 59 is a timeline of Pasteur's life and work.

Enquiry: How did surgery improve in the nineteenth century?

Students' Book pp. 134–139
Worksheets 60, 61, 62, 63

The advances in surgery 1750–1900 were dependent on developments in the control of pain, the staunching of bleeding and the removal of the risk of infection. **Worksheet 60** sets out these issues around the picture of the operation in 1800.

Pages 135–139 then take each of the three key areas of pain, infection and bleeding in turn which is the simplest way of covering developments, although students should be reminded about how much easier it is to view a development in hindsight.

One of the features of the history of medicine which students find hardest to appreciate when we have the benefit of hindsight is the opposition which new developments often provoked. We have emphasised this 'opposition' theme throughout the nineteenth century (see also smallpox, antiseptics, public health, etc.).

(Pages 135–136)
The problem of pain

Task: Worksheet 61 provides a framework for the Task on page 136.

(Pages 137–139)
Infection

For the **Activity** on page 139, use **Worksheet 62** to record the arguments for and against Lister's methods. Linking the discovery of germ theory and changes in surgical practice is important and requires a clear framework for the sequence of events.

For the **Task** on page 139 **Worksheet 63** provides a timeline (1850–1900) that links germ theory and developments in surgical practice. Students should start by completing key dates in the career of Lister and for improvements in surgery. This information can then be transferred to the timeline where the various developments need to be linked: for example, those associated with pain, infection and bleeding.

Enquiry: Why were sewers and water supply improved in the nineteenth century?

Students' Book pp. 140–147
Worksheets 64, 65, 66, 67, 68, 69, 70, 71

In this enquiry students will trace the changes in public health during the century and examine the changing attitudes towards the provision of public health facilities.

There has been considerable debate about the relative importance of the public health movement in reducing mortality in nineteenth-century Britain. Most recently, historians of the social history of medicine have concluded that the role of public health was particularly important in the last two decades of the century. They have highlighted the effects of a fresh water supply and an adequate sewage system on general health, especially in the large towns. Also of significance was the improved diet enjoyed by a greater proportion of the population as well as better housing. One area that is difficult to quantify and to find evidence for is domestic hygiene. A number of studies indicate that this factor was especially important as health education and knowledge improved.

Students will need to be reminded that the enquiry goes back a few decades from the previous one – before Pasteur's germ theory when people still did not understand the causes of the disease.

Worksheet 64 is a play which has been effectively used over a number of years to introduce students to the fear which cholera produced in the early nineteenth century, and to its causes and treatments. It could be read through in class before tackling the enquiry on pages 140–144.

(Pages 140–141)
The battle over public health

Worksheet 65 is a copy of the cartoon 'A Court for King Cholera' from *Punch*. The cartoon brings together many of the public health nuisances that were recognised by people at the time. Students can use the drawing to label and annotate the contemporary, stereotypical view of a poor area of a growing town. Cholera, described as a shock disease by Anthony Wohl in his excellent book *Endangered Lives*, stirred many local authorities into action. However, their efforts often lasted only as long as the duration of the scare. The attitudes illustrated in **Sources 4–8** on page 141 partly explain why the provision of public health facilities was not seen by everyone as the way to prevent disease spreading.

Worksheet 66 is a copy of the table that will enable students to compare attitudes to the Black Death with those seen in the responses to cholera.

(Pages 142–143)
Discovering the causes of cholera – the work of John Snow

The classic case study that resulted in the causes of cholera being observed was undertaken by John Snow in Soho in 1854. Snow did not know about germs and bacteria but he was able to observe the onset of the disease and its spread. The case study illustrates the meticulous observation and recording by Snow. It also shows the sophistication of the statistical analysis.

(Page 144)
Why were public health reforms begun?

It is often assumed that ill health was confined to the towns. This was not the case. Conditions in many rural areas were as bad if not worse than in some urban areas.

Worksheet 67 uses the two cartoons, 'A Court for King Cholera' and 'The Cottage'. Students can use these drawings to compare the conditions as interpreted by cartoonists at the time. The cartoons come from *Punch* when it was a satirical magazine with some hard-hitting social comment. Bound copies of *Punch* can be bought quite cheaply from secondhand book shops. This would be a good opportunity to highlight the advantages and disadvantages of using cartoons as historical evidence. The common problems can be recorded in the boxes.

The battle over public health was a major issue in many towns. It was not until the 1880s that the majority of towns accepted that public health facilities should be provided as a matter of course. Until then, there had been a natural reluctance on the part of ratepayers to fund the cost of building water supply and sewage disposal systems. It is worth looking at contemporary local newspapers for reports of the debates between those who wanted change and the 'dirty party'.

(Page 145)
Why was there opposition to public health reforms?

There was considerable opposition to public health reforms at all levels. Students need to appreciate the cost of the public health schemes. It is worth seeking out some local sources from your record office or local studies library. Some facsimile documents are published in the John Murray Public Record Office Sourcebook, *Expansion of Trade and Industry*.

(Page 146)
Why was public health finally improved?

Final acceptance of the need to provide public health facilities did not come till well after the passing of the Public Health Act of 1875.

Worksheets 68 and 69 are alternative approaches to helping students interrelate the reasons why public health was improved.

Worksheet 70 provides a framework for the essay that asks students to agree or disagree with the statement 'It was impossible to make real improvements in public health in Britain before 1861.'

(Page 147)
Public health is more than sewers and water!

The public health movement at the end of the century was not limited to the provision of clean water and sewage. Other aspects are covered on page 147. Students are encouraged to research one or more of these themes.

Worksheet 71 provides a table on which they can record their findings. Researching these topics will require local or national sources. It is worth collecting a pack of materials for each of these themes from either local or nationally available sources and publishers.

Enquiry: A century of medical progress?

Students' Book p. 148
Worksheets 72, 73, 74

Bringing together the developments of the nineteenth century requires students to categorise the areas where developments took place.

Task: Worksheet 72 is a copy of the chart with space for students to make notes.

Worksheet 73 is an extension activity for the most able that looks at possible hypotheses for explaining progress in this period.

Activity: Worksheet 74 is our version of the jigsaw. There are no 'right' answers of course, although there are some wrong ones! The purpose of our chart is to compare with students' ideas. It can also be used to support students who need it, and to bypass the potentially time-consuming drawing. If you white out the labels on the jigsaw pieces before copying, then all students need to do is add their own labels.

Thackray Medical Museum

A new resource for nineteenth- and twentieth-century medicine is the Thackray Medical Museum, opening in April 1997. The museum covers public health issues, the development of germ theory, vaccines and chemical drugs, and surgical developments from pre-anaesthetic operations to the latest techniques. The museum can be used to gather information, to revise topics interactively, with, for example, students choosing from a wide range of 1840s treatments before discovering their fate. For more information contact:

The Thackray Medical Museum
131 Becket Street
Leeds LS9 7LP

Telephone 0113 244 4343

Chapter 5: Medicine and health in the twentieth century

Enquiry: Why has medicine and health improved so rapidly since 1900?

Students' Book p. 149

This century, especially the years after 1945, has seen massive changes in all aspects of medicine and health. In 1900, for the majority of the population, health and medical care was much improved compared with that in 1800. However, although doctors may have been able to explain the causes of many common diseases they were still unable to cure the majority of them. Again students need to be reminded of the timelag between:

- understanding the causes of diseases,
- the ability to prevent them and
- the capacity to cure the patient.

Many of the scientific discoveries of the nineteenth century had laid the foundations of what was to come next: the ability to cure patients, through surgery or the administration of drugs.

Enquiry: What medical progress did the First World War bring about?

Students' Book pp. 150–153
Worksheets 75, 76

The First World War had considerable impact on health and medicine. Aspects of the impact of the war are illustrated in **Source 1**. The case study on pages 151–153 concentrates on surgery.

Question 1: Worksheet 75 provides a framework to record the experience of the wounded Blake Sullivan.

Task: Worksheet 76: A critical judgement of the impact of the First World War is required at the end of the section on page 153. A framework for the answer is provided on this worksheet.

Enquiry: The fight against infection: from magic bullets to guided missiles

Students' Book pp. 154–155
Worksheet 77

This spread illustrates the two lines of research that proved successful in preventing and curing many diseases. Once again the processes of the

research are shown in graphical form for greater clarity. **Worksheet 77** reproduces **Source 1** with blank word bubbles so that students can complete them. It should be remembered that there is a considerable gap between the discoveries made by Pasteur and Koch and the production of the first magic bullet for general usage in the mid 1930s. Students should be reminded that the development of drugs and cures did not follow simple, regular, logical steps. Many research scientists at the end of the 1920s doubted that any new magic bullets would be discovered. Two factors that broke the research deadlock in the early 1930s were, first, the development of the electron microscope and, secondly, the impact of the resources from pharmaceutical companies and their research teams.

Enquiry: Case study: the development of penicillin

Students' Book pp. 156–159
Worksheets 78, 79

The story of penicillin is fascinating not just because of the medical breakthrough that it represented but the interesting politics that surrounded its development.

(Page 159)
Penicillin – why then?
Task: Question 3 is a favourite exam question as it clearly shows a range of factors working together. **Worksheet 78** helps to record the factor which was of most importance at each stage of the development of penicillin. It will help provide students with an overview so they can answer Question 3.

Worksheet 79 is an account by Howard Florey of the discovery of penicillin. This is a complex text for students at this level but it is worth using in part if not as a whole. It can be used as an extended piece of work to help students answer the questions in the Task.

Genetic engineering
You could organise a class debate on the ethics of genetic engineering based on the proposition 'We believe everyone should have the right to choose perfect children.'

Enquiry: Why did infant mortality decrease so rapidly from 1900 to 1945?

Students' Book pp. 160–162
Worksheets 80A, 80B, 81

Infant mortality is a key indicator of the health and welfare of a nation. In 1900 it was clear that the most vulnerable group in society, the under fives, was no more likely to live beyond the age of five than youngsters of the same age in 1800. Yet in the next 50 years infant mortality plunged.

Historians have found it difficult to be precise about the reasons for this decline but there is evidence that points towards a significant improvement in domestic hygiene and child care skills. This question is still open to debate and research. Certainly the government started to fund both of these areas in the years before the First World War. The government's motives had much to do with building a healthy competitive nation and reflect the influence of the Eugenics movement. **Sources 4–10** identify a number of the measures taken by the government and give a range of statistics.

(Pages 160–161)
Source 3: Although two items are not given as quotes but as authors' text, they were still used as explanations at the time – we just could not find a snappy quote.
    Question 3: Stage 1 should be to list the common factors identified by these explanations. **Worksheets 80A and 80B** help students do this.
    Question 4: Students should choose three problems to tackle *not* three explanations.

(Page 162)
Task: Worksheet 81 provides a framework for the essay question 'Why did infant mortality decline so rapidly from 1900 to 1945?'

Enquiry: What was the impact of the Second World War on medicine and health in Britain?

Students' Book p. 163
Worksheet 82

This page brings together information about the impact of the Second World War on health and medicine. It is intended to be a summary; more detailed information about some of the themes can be found elsewhere in this book:

■ drugs, pages 156–159
■ hygiene, pages 161–162
■ NHS, pages 164–169.

Task: Worksheet 82 provides a chart for students to complete.

Enquiry: 'From cradle to grave' – The National Health Service

Students' Book pp. 164–169
Worksheets 83, 84

Pages 164–165 look at the gradual acceptance by the government that health insurance could not be left to the individual and the free market. The changes in the 1930s brought the system as it existed close to collapse with the majority of the population without access to the necessary medical care. Page 165 highlights yet again the limited funds available for health care and the vital role played by women.

(Pages 168–169)
Why did people oppose the NHS?
Activity: Worksheet 83 is a template for recording points to use in the discussion on page 168.

Achievements of the NHS
Worksheet 84 is a template for the **Task** on page 169 – helping students set out the features of health care before and after 1948.

Enquiry: What kills people today?

Students' Book pp. 170–171

There is sometimes an assumption that medical science can solve any problem, given time. This has been challenged by the emergence of new epidemics and the reappearance of some of the old 'killer' diseases. This section looks at the changing patterns of illness by comparing 1919 with 1992: 1919 has been chosen because it is the first date for which a broad range of statistics is available. It would be helpful to have a range of recent health literature and posters for this enquiry. The best source for this material is the local health centre.

Enquiry: AIDS: the 'charter disease'

Students' Book p. 172
Worksheets 85, 86

The reactions of governments and individuals to AIDS tells us a lot about human nature and the difficulties of coping with a threatening epidemic.

Worksheet 85 provides a framework for comparing the attitudes and beliefs of people to AIDS and the Black Death or cholera.

Worksheet 86 contains two additional contemporary sources. If you are using this course in future years you may find more up-to-date alternatives if these health problems have abated once again.

Enquiry: Why has surgery developed so rapidly in recent years?

Students' Book pp. 173–174

The greatest revolution in medical care for ordinary people has taken place since the Second World War.

Source 2 offers a few examples of developments that have occurred since 1945. We are only able to give a glimpse of developments in an ever-evolving discipline. Students could add many others by their own research.

(Page 174)
Questions 1 and 2 will be ideal for class debate or discussion which could be set up as a wider ranging discussion into medical ethics embracing more diverse topics such as:

- genetic engineering (page 159)
- drug development (page 159)
- private v. public funding of health care (page 169)
- the cost of AIDS research (page 172)
- alternative medicine (page 175)
- global concerns (page 177)
- issues on page 179.

Enquiry: What is alternative medicine?

Students' Book p. 175

Alternative medicine embraces many disciplines. Some of these are ancient and have been practised throughout history. Others are more recent. There are very different opinions within the medical profession about alternative medicine and this is a fertile area for debate. An excellent résumé is *Alternative Medicine in Britain*, ed. Mike Saks (OUP, 1992). This anthology provides both an historical perspective and a range of contemporary viewpoints including the text of the BMA's (critical) report on alternative medicine

prepared in the 1980s, the riposte to the BMA by the British Holistic Medical Association, and a case study on acupuncture.

Leaflets on alternative medicine can be found for use as contemporary source material. For example, branches of Boots the Chemist have leaflets about both homeopathy and herbalism. Most bookshops have stacks of books on alternative medicine. You can put together a small pack with the help of the class.

Question 1: Alternative medicine is also known by some as holistic medicine or complementary medicine.

Enquiry: Has public health improved during the twentieth century?

Students' Book pp. 176–177
Worksheet 87

Many of the nineteenth-century targets of the public health movement were met. However, some public health problems were never tackled. We focus on two of them.

Healthier housing

Activity: Worksheet 87 brings together some of the improvements in housing provision during this century.

Enquiry: Why are people in some countries healthier than in others?

Students' Book p. 178
Worksheet 88

Most of the changes described in Chapter 5 have benefited a small minority of the world's population. The **Task** looks at the problems facing the developing world and those that faced Britain in the last century.

Worksheet 88 will help to structure and record this enquiry in continuity and change.

Twentieth-century medicine: conclusions

Students' Book p. 179
Worksheets 89, 90, 91

This penultimate section in Chapter 5 asks students to take an overview of twentieth-century medicine. The Tasks challenge students with a series of structured questions concluding with a requirement to make an informed comment about whether there are limits to progress.

Task 1: Worksheets 89 and 90 provide frameworks to help students structure their note-taking and answers. Worksheet 89 can be copied to A3 size.

Task 2: Worksheet 91 provides help with answering **Question 1**.

The health jigsaw AD2000

Students' Book p. 180
Worksheet 92

The jigsaw at the end of this chapter brings together the developments in the history of medicine. At this point students should be able to look back and begin to discuss the development of medicine and health from the basis of both a sound knowledge of the subject and an understanding of the trends and turning points. Chapter 6 will reinforce this ability to take the long view over time.

For many years the history of medicine was dominated by the work of doctors who wrote with passion about their view of the development of medicine and the central role of the medical profession. In recent years historians have stood back from this interpretation and questioned the view that doctors were primarily responsible for developments and improvements in medical care.

■ **Question 3: Worksheet 92** provides a framework for students' answers.

Chapter 6: Conclusions: explaining change and continuity in medicine and health

This chapter gives students the chance to focus on the conceptual issues that will be at the heart of assessment. At the same time they will have the chance to revise content because there is little new material in Chapter 6. We decided to revisit material because asking students to get to grips with new content would distract from the need to tackle the key concepts of the development study. Throughout the chapter, students are encouraged to look back into the narrative section to find further evidence to support their conclusions. Timelines provide relevant page references. A further objective of this chapter is to reinforce students' understanding of the sequence of events through regular repetition of that sequence.

Enquiry: How have methods of treatment changed through history?

Students' Book pp. 182–183
Worksheet 93

This summary spread provides students with an overview of treatments and of the sequence of periods they have studied. Teachers may wish to tackle the questions orally or in writing.

Questions 1, 3 and 5: The answers can be found in the timeline but students should be able to bring their knowledge to bear on answering the other questions. Note that trephining is shown here as a prehistoric treatment but it continued to be used across the centuries and some very ornate trephining tools used in the nineteenth century can be seen in museums. A photograph of trephining tools is shown in **Source 9**, page 210. Trephining has also been used (sometimes self-inflicted) in recent years.

Worksheet 93 provides a copy of the illustrated timeline on pages 182–183 of the Students' Book.

Enquiry: How has understanding of the causes of disease changed through history?

Students' Book pp. 184–185

This spread has similar objectives to the previous topic – presenting a simple overview as a springboard for discussion and again reinforcing knowledge of chronology. The idea

of causes can be linked back to the jigsaws at the end of each previous chapter where only the most recent doctor could complete the jigsaw once germ theory had been discovered. Note the overlap of beliefs, with some continuing amongst many people even though scientists had made a theoretical breakthrough. Refer back, for example, to the use of mice as a cure (page 21) in twentieth-century Britain.

Enquiry: Why? The factors that have caused change and continuity in medicine and health

Students' Book pp. 186–187
Worksheets 94, 95

Page 186 summarises the way factors or causes can work together to produce or prevent change while the picture on page 186 shows the factors that have appeared in the narrative.

Worksheet 94 can be used as a template for various questions.

Students could try to tackle **Questions 1–3** on page 187 from memory or use their factors grids to suggest answers. **Worksheet 95** provides a chart for students to record their answers. This page and its questions could be returned to when students have reached the end of this section (up to and including page 198) to see whether they have changed their conclusions.

Enquiry: Factor 1: Governments

Students' Book pp. 188–189

This spread and the two that follow on, religion and war, have the same format. Each provides a range of material that will enable students to start thinking about the questions but they can also use the timeline indexes to seek out more examples. The examples on each spread represent most major periods but limitations of space mean that not all are represented by sources.

Government was chosen as the first example of a factor because the role of governments has been extensively covered in Chapters 4 and 5 and so the issues may still be fresh in students' minds. It will be more difficult for students to identify the absence of government actions – the beginning of Chapter 2 will help in this.

Questions 4 and 5: Students could refer to their factors grids or to the picture on page 187 for ideas. The most obvious examples are the public health revolution in the late nineteenth century, the development of drugs such as penicillin, and the setting up of the NHS in the twentieth century.

Enquiry: Factor 2: Religion

Students' Book pp. 190–191

Religion here encompasses a wide range of beliefs. In contrast to governments, this topic provides clearer examples of the way change was prevented or inhibited. Again students can use the timeline index to search for more examples, either individually or with pairs working on different periods so that the whole class more rapidly builds up the list required for **Question 2**.

Enquiry: Factor 3: War

Students' Book pp. 192–193
Worksheet 96

This spread is more adventurous in encouraging students to think of their own questions, having worked on the previous two topics. A list of questions to answer could be compiled on the board from students' suggestions and then re-sorted into the best order. Alternatively **Worksheet 96** contains a list of questions for students to tackle.

Having looked at governments, religion and war, students could now consider which factor they think has been the most important in the history of medicine. It is better to do this here, juggling and comparing three factors, than to do a similar exercise after looking at more factors.

Enquiry: The role of individuals

Students' Book p. 194
Worksheets 97, 98, 99

This page and the accompanying worksheets provide revision of chronology as well as work on the role of individuals.

Worksheets 97 and 99 can be duplicated and cut up, so that students can undertake sequencing exercises by moving the pictures around into the right order. These, if enlarged, could also form the basis of a timeline on the wall. If a class timeline is constructed on the

wall, then pairs of students could be given responsibility for producing the notes to accompany each individual on the timeline.

Questions 1 and 2: For ease of reference the individuals on Worksheet 97 are:

- Fleming (page 156)
- Harvey (pages 88–89)
- Lister (pages 138–139)
- Pasteur (pages 128–129, 131–132)
- Hippocrates (pages 29, 32–33)
- Garrett (pages 124–125).

Questions 3 and 4: Worksheet 98 is a copy of the timeline.

Enquiry: What other factors have affected medicine and health?

Students' Book p. 195

The roles of these factors also need some discussion as students may encounter them in examinations or other assessments. This page can only show a few examples but others are listed in the box.

Enquiry: How did different factors work together to produce change?

Students' Book pp. 196–197
Worksheets 100, 101

Work on the individual factors and in the narrative should have prepared students to look at the complexities of causation. This example revisits a topic already studied, to reinforce content knowledge and to focus on the way factors worked together. The chart on page 197 shows a wide range of links.

Worksheet 100 is an arrowless version of this chart. It could be used first with students, asking them to draw in arrows to show links. Then their ideas could be compared with the chart on page 197. Students could then explain the links by jotting brief notes next to the arrows on their chart (**Task 1, Question 1**).

Task 2: Worksheet 101 provides a similar chart but teachers wanting students to research the topic could give them a grid with blank boxes or with only some of the boxes labelled.

Enquiry: How did different factors work together to prevent change?

Students' Book p. 198
Worksheet 102

Explaining continuity is usually more difficult than explaining change. This page repeats the previous exercise but looking at why there was continuity.

Questions 1 and 2: Worksheet 102 provides a copy of the chart for students to annotate. Again some students will be able to tackle this exercise using only a set of blank boxes, working out for themselves the relevant factors from Chapter 2.

Enquiry: Continuity: the use of herbs as medicines

Students' Book p. 200

Herbal remedies provide an obvious example of continuity, with plentiful references in the narrative section. It will be important to emphasise that herbs still play an important role in treatments as price lists or catalogues from any health food shop will reveal.

Question 4: Note the evidence in the sections on Egyptian treatments and medieval treatments that herbal remedies often did work.

Enquiry: The leech makes a comeback

Students' Book p. 201

The material on the leech provides more content to illustrate how an idea or treatment can come back into fashion. There is now at least one leech farm whose business is to supply leeches to scientists and doctors for the treatments described on this page.

Enquiry: Change and continuity – women's role as midwives

Students' Book pp. 202–203
Worksheet 103

This is a more self-contained study, investigating a complex pattern of change and continuity. Students could construct a timeline, listing above the line examples of women's role in midwifery and below the line times when women were excluded or played an inferior role. This will allow students to see the pattern before explaining to them why these changes took place.

Worksheet 103 provides the basis for **Task 2**.

Enquiry: Progress and regress: the story of public health

Students' Book pp. 204–205
Worksheet 104

Sources 1–8 will enable students to tackle **Question 1** but this outline list can be added to by pairs of students researching different periods for further examples. The timeline index will direct them to relevant material. If this information is then recorded on a timeline (progress above, regress below the line) or in a chronological list (different columns for progress and regress) students will easily be able to see the pattern for answers to **Questions 2 and 3**.

Question 4 can be tackled at different levels according to the sophistication of students' ideas. Graph C reflects the pattern of public health for the richer elements of society but some students may be aware that Graph B is a better reflection of the pattern for the poor.

Worksheet 104 provides the basis for **Task 2** on page 205.

Enquiry: Turning points: the consequences of germ theory

Students' Book pp. 206–207
Worksheet 105

The text on page 206 shows one approach to explaining what a turning point is. Students are likely to be much more riveted by turning points in their teacher's life if you are prepared to provide them with a snippet from your life story.

Task: Question 1 will start to get students thinking and identifying turning points in medicine before moving on to the other questions.

Question 4: Worksheet 105 provides an essay outline for this question.

Enquiry: Patterns of change and continuity: surgery through time

Students' Book pp. 208–210

Surgery, as well as being interesting because of the blood and gore involved, provides a good core study for pulling together the conceptual themes of Chapter 6. It is a mini-development study of its own. Students will first need to draw up a list of the different aspects of surgery. These could be recorded chronologically and set in columns. Students could begin by rewording information from the sources on this spread and then add more using the timeline index. It is important in this final exercise that students do not just deal with the techniques of surgery but explicitly describe patterns of change and continuity, turning points and the causes of change and continuity.

What progress?

Prehistory

The ancient civilisations of Egypt, Greece and Rome
The first doctors

Life expectancy: women 38; men 40

The Middle Ages (AD500–1400)
Very little medical progress

Life expectancy: women 36; men 37

The Medical Renaissance (AD1400–1700)
Many new discoveries about the body

Life expectancy: women 38; men 41

The eighteenth and nineteenth centuries
Discoveries about the true causes of disease

Life expectancy: women 49; men 45

The twentieth century
Rapid progress in preventing and curing many diseases

Life expectancy: women 78; men 72

Medicine & Health Through Time

Explanations of disease through time

What is a development study?

Use this worksheet to answer questions 1 and 3 on page 5.

1. What ideas did the people in column A have about the causes of disease? Fill in column B with the captions from Source 2 on pages 4 and 5 of your book. One group of people might have had more than one idea about the causes of disease.
2. How did they treat illnesses? Now fill in column C, linking treatments (Source 3, page 5) to the peoples in Column A.

A	B	C
Prehistory		
The ancient civilisations of Egypt, Greece and Rome The first doctors Life expectancy: women 38; men 40		
The Middle Ages Very little medical progress Life expectancy: women 36; men 37		

A	B	C

The Medical Renaissance
Many new discoveries about the body

Life expectancy: women 38; men 41

The eighteenth and nineteenth centuries
Discoveries about the true causes of disease

Life expectancy: women 49; men 45

The twentieth century
Rapid progress in preventing and curing many diseases

Life expectancy: women 78; men 72

How healthy were the people of Isbister?

Use this worksheet to answer question 2 on page 8.

	Isbister 3000BC
1. How healthy were people?	
2. What caused sickness?	
3. How did they treat illnesses and injuries?	
4. Who provided medical care?	
5. What did they think caused illness?	

Evidence from Isbister

Accidents rarely caused death. Only 2 per cent of the people had broken bones and most of them showed evidence of healing. Prehistoric Orkney seems to have been peaceful. No fortifications or weapons have been found.

The people had strong muscles, especially leg muscles. Some of their ankle bones were unusual, probably because they did a lot of climbing with their ankles flexed to collect birds' eggs from the cliffs for food.

Men were 160cm to 172cm tall. Their average height was 170cm. Women were from 146cm to 162cm. Their average height was 161cm.

There was a high death-rate among babies and young children, and also between the ages of 20 and 35. Very few people lived to be over 40.

Their teeth were very healthy, although they were ground down by particles of stone which got into bread when the corn was ground. Only nine out of 1,537 teeth had decay. However, a man aged 45–50 had three abscesses on his back teeth which must have been extremely painful.

Women died younger than men. Most women died between the ages of 15 and 24. This pattern is found in almost all pre-industrial societies from prehistoric times to the present. The likely reasons are the strains of pregnancy and childbirth, poor diet and the demands of heavy physical work.

Most people suffered osteoarthritis – painful swelling of the joints. Nearly half the adults suffered from it at young ages and even children's skeletons showed signs of osteoarthritis. It may have been caused by carrying or pulling heavy loads which were fixed by a strap or rope running across the neck and under the opposite armpit. This was a common method of carrying burdens in Orkney up to recent times.

How healthy were people in prehistoric Britain?

Use this worksheet to answer the Activity on page 13.

A	B	C
	The best type of evidence to support this statement comes from:	Other evidence to support the statement in column A is:
1.		
2.		
3.		
4.		
5.		
6.		
7.		

Could prehistoric healers help the sick?

Use the outline on this worksheet to help you answer question 3 on page 13. Use each sentence to begin a new paragraph.

■ When prehistoric people were sick they could go to different kinds of healers.

_____

_____

_____

_____

_____

■ Prehistoric people believed that many diseases were caused by spirits.

_____

_____

_____

_____

_____

■ Some illnesses were treated with charms and magic. Other illnesses were treated with herbs or practical remedies.

_____

_____

_____

_____

_____

■ There was no way of stopping pain.

_____

_____

_____

_____

_____

■ The evidence for prehistoric medicine helps to answer some questions but we cannot find definite answers for other questions.

_____

_____

_____

_____

_____

Egypt, Greece and Rome: the great empires

This worksheet gives you a copy of the timeline on pages 14–15.

1. Shade in each of the empires, copying the timeline in your textbook.
2. Add the labels from your textbook.

	3000BC	2000BC	1000BC	0	500AD
BRITAIN					
EGYPTIAN EMPIRE					
GREEK EMPIRE					
ROMAN EMPIRE					

Medicine & Health Through Time

How did life in Egypt affect medicine?

Use this worksheet to answer the Activity on page 16.

Medicine & Health Through Time

Egyptian medicine

Use this worksheet to answer the Activity on page 19.

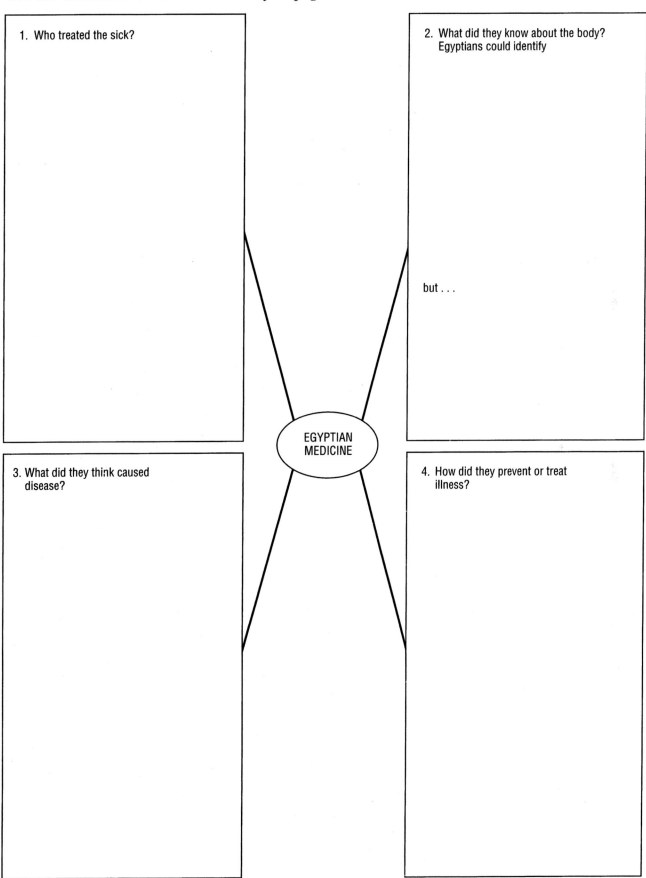

1. Who treated the sick?

2. What did they know about the body?
   Egyptians could identify

   but . . .

EGYPTIAN
MEDICINE

3. What did they think caused
   disease?

4. How did they prevent or treat
   illness?

Egyptian medicine

Use this outline to answer the Task on page 22.

■ Egyptians used ideas and methods that were used by prehistoric peoples:
magical treatments, the belief that gods and spirits caused illnesses, herbs as medicines,
priests or medicine men as healers.

_____

_____

_____

_____

_____

_____

_____

_____

■ However, the Egyptians also had new ideas and methods:
doctors, metal surgical instruments, new knowledge of anatomy, doctors looked for logical
causes of disease.

_____

_____

_____

_____

_____

_____

_____

■ The changes were important for the future because . . .

_____

_____

_____

_____

_____

_____

_____

_____

Were there medical developments in other places?

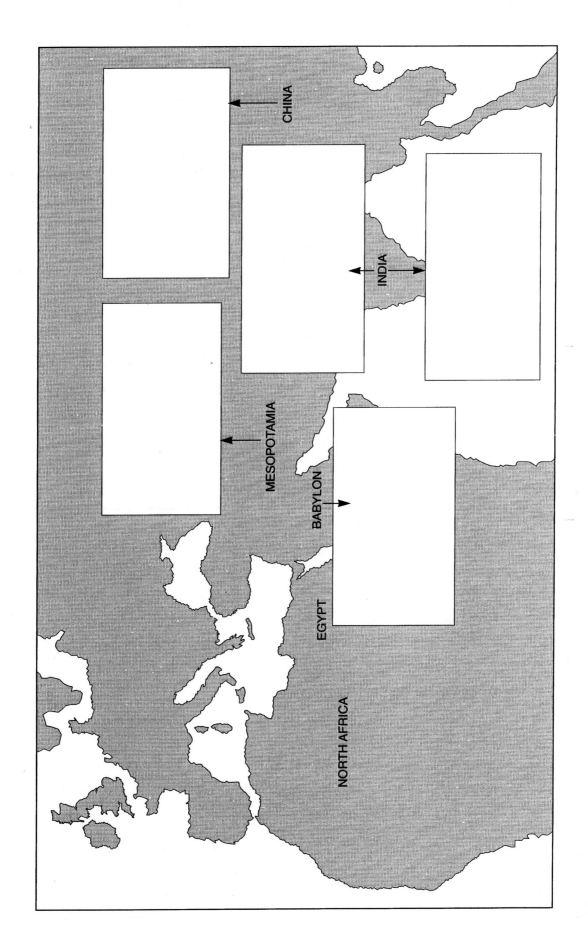

CHINA

INDIA

MESOPOTAMIA

BABYLON

EGYPT

NORTH AFRICA

Could women become doctors in ancient Greece?

Use this worksheet with Source 3 on page 29.

Hagnodice was not allowed to become a doctor because she was a woman. However, she disguised herself as a man, trained as a doctor and treated many patients. Then her city's rulers discovered she was a woman. How would Hagnodice have answered these questions from the city's rulers?

■ How did you learn about medicine?

_____

_____

_____

_____

_____

_____

_____

■ Why did you trick Herophilus?

_____

_____

_____

_____

_____

_____

■ Why did you want to be a doctor?

_____

_____

_____

_____

_____

■ Why should we change the law to let you be a doctor?

_____

_____

_____

_____

_____

_____

_____

'Best amputate, whilst he has some strength'

Use this worksheet for the Activity on page 37.

SOURCE 1 From *The Silver Pigs* by Lindsey Davis (reproduced with permission from Pan Books)

❝ I was lying on a high, hard bed in a small, square room at a legionary hospital. Unhurried footsteps sometimes paced the long corridor round the courtyard at the back of the administration block. I recognized the evil reek of antiseptic turpentine. I felt the reassuring pressure of neat, firm bandaging. I was warm. I was clean. I was resting in tranquillity in a quiet, caring place ...

Their opium had ebbed away. When I moved pain shot back. A red tunic, brooched on one shoulder with the medical snake and staff, loomed over me, then sheered off again when I stared him in the eye. I recognized the complete absence of bedside manner: must be the chief (medical) orderly. Pupils stretched their necks behind him like awestruck ducklings jostling their mother duck.

'Tell me the truth, Hippocrates!' I jested. They never tell you the truth.

He tickled me up and down my ribs like a moneychanger on an abacus. I yelped, though not because his hands were cold.

'Still in discomfort – that will last several months. He can expect a great deal of pain. No real problems if he avoids getting pneumonia ...' He sounded disappointed at the thought that I might. 'Emaciated specimen; he's vulnerable to gangrene in this leg.' My heart sank. 'Best amputate, whilst he has some strength.' I glared at him with a heartbreak that brightened him up. 'We can give him something!' he consoled his listeners. Did you know, the main part of a surgeon's training is how to ignore the screams? ...

The surgeon was called Simplex ... Simplex had spent fourteen years in the army. He could calm a sixteen-year-old soldier with an arrow shot into his head. He could seal blisters, dose dysentery, bathe eyes, even deliver babies from the wives the legionaries were not supposed to have. He was bored with all that. I was his favourite patient now. Among his set of spatulas, scalpels, probes, shears, and forceps, he owned a shiny great mallet big enough to bash in fencing stakes. Its use in surgery was for amputations, driving home his chisel through soldiers' joints. He had the chisel and the saw too: a complete toolbag, all laid out on a table by my bed.

They drugged me, but not enough. Flavius Hilaris wished me luck, then slipped out of the room. I don't blame him. If I hadn't been strapped down to the bed with four six-foot set-faced cavalrymen grappling my shoulders and feet, I would have shot straight out after him ...

'Stop it at once!' cried Helena Justina. I had no idea when she came in. I had not realized she was there. 'There's no gangrene!' stormed the senator's daughter. She seemed to lose her temper wherever she was. 'I would expect an army surgeon to know – gangrene has its own distinctive smell. Didius Falco's feet may be cheesy, but they're not that bad!' Wonderful woman; an informer in trouble could always count on her. 'He has chilblains. In Britain that's nothing to wonder at – all he needs for those is a hot turnip mash! Pull his leg as straight as you can, then leave him alone; the poor man has suffered enough!'

I passed out with relief. ❞

Medicine & Health Through Time

Were Roman medical ideas the same as those of the Greeks?

Use this worksheet for the Activity on page 40.

Aspects of Greek medicine	Did the Romans use this idea or method – a lot – a little – not at all	Example
1. Gods could cure illnesses and injuries.		
2. Doctors observed patients and recorded symptoms.		
3. Herbs were commonly used as treatments.		
4. Doctors frequently recommended exercise and changes in diet.		
5. Doctors successfully carried out simple operations.		
6. Doctors were very interested in discovering the causes of disease.		

New Roman ideas:

_____

_____

_____

_____

_____

_____

_____

The Emperor's doctor

Use this worksheet for the Activity on page 45.

Name _____

Age _____ **Place of birth** _____

Education

_____
_____
_____
_____

Work

_____
_____
_____
_____
_____

List your greatest medical achievements:

_____
_____
_____
_____
_____
_____
_____
_____

Why are you the best candidate for the post of doctor to the Emperor?

_____
_____
_____
_____
_____
_____
_____
_____
_____
_____

What was the Romans' big idea?

Use this worksheet to complete the Activity on page 47.

- Tick which of these people you are:
  a) a wealthy Roman citizen ☐
  b) a soldier serving in Wroxeter in Britain ☐
  c) a poor person living in Rome. ☐

- Do you have a fresh water supply?

_____

_____

_____

_____

_____

- Do you go to the baths?

_____

_____

_____

_____

_____

- Do drains and sewers take away refuse?

_____

_____

_____

_____

_____

- Do you use a private toilet or a public toilet?

_____

_____

_____

_____

_____

- How do your facilities compare with those of other people?

_____

_____

_____

_____

_____

Was Roman medicine the same as Greek medicine?

Use this worksheet to help with the Task on page 47. The statements below can be used as the opening sentences of each paragraph of your essay. How would you complete each paragraph?

■ Both the Greeks and the Romans believed that gods could cure sickness.

_____
_____
_____
_____
_____

■ Greek and Roman doctors used many of the same methods and cures.

_____
_____
_____
_____
_____

■ However, Galen used new treatments based on his theory of opposites.

_____
_____
_____
_____
_____

■ Greek doctors were more interested in learning about the causes of disease than many Roman doctors.

_____
_____
_____
_____
_____

■ The Romans' main medical improvement was in public health.

_____
_____
_____
_____
_____

Medicine & Health Through Time

Did the Romans have new ideas?

Use this worksheet to complete the Task on page 48.

1. People continued to believe in the power of the gods of healing. Even Galen acted on messages in dreams.

2. Herbs and plants continued to be the basis for cures, as they had been for generations.

3. Roman doctors added little to the methods and theories they inherited from the Greeks; although Galen made important discoveries about anatomy.

4. Public health schemes were developed to prevent disease and were particularly valuable in the army.

Change and continuity in Roman Britain

Study the sources below and then complete the Activity.

SOURCE 1 Is this what happened to the Celts after the Romans arrived in Britain? Did everyone become Romanised, speaking Latin, wearing togas and living longer, healthier lives? Or was there little change for most Britons?

During the Roman period Britain's population reached more than 5 million. This was probably the result of people being healthier.

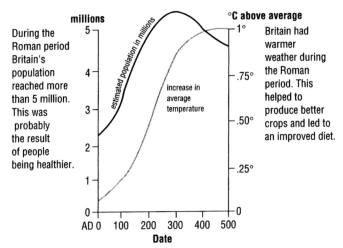

Britain had warmer weather during the Roman period. This helped to produce better crops and led to an improved diet.

SOURCE 2 The population and temperature of Roman Britain

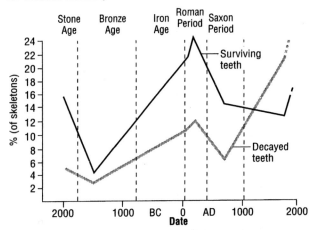

SOURCE 4 How good were teeth? This evidence comes from skeletons investigated by archaeologists

Doctors
Each legion of the army had its own doctors who also treated local people. Some of them settled in Britain when they retired.

Improved treatments
Army doctors collected treatments and herbal remedies from around the Roman Empire and took them to new places, including Britain.

Public health
The Romans built sewers and water supplies in towns where army legions were based such as York and Cirencester.

SOURCE 3 The influence of the Roman army on health in Britain. Members of the army and wealthy Britons living in towns benefited most from these changes

	Men	Women
Pre-Roman (Iron Age)	167.8cm	n/a
Roman	170.2cm	156.3cm

S**OURCE 5** How tall were people? The evidence comes from skeletons found in York and Cirencester. Increased height is usually a sign of a better diet

S**OURCE 6** How long did people live? These figures are based on evidence from skeletons and tombstones. The Cirencester figure is based on 299 skeletons. They probably included both rich and poor. Cirencester was a flourishing place with all the improved facilities you would expect in a Roman town

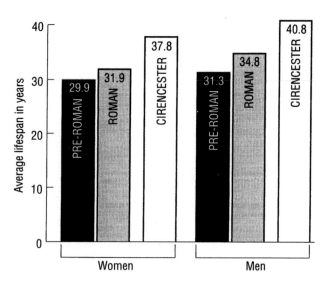

■ ACTIVITY

This is a discussion Activity. Work in groups of six, each member of the group taking one of the roles below. Work out which of your characters would probably have lived longest in Roman Britain, and why. Sources 1–6 give you background information about Roman Britain. Pages 49–51 of the Students' Book give you much more detail.

a) a centurion in the Roman legion based at York, one of the most important towns in Roman Britain

b) a merchant living in Cirencester

c) the merchant's wife

d) the merchant's slave

e) a farmer living in northern Britain

f) the farmer's wife

Would you survive in ancient Rome?

Use this worksheet to play the game on page 51.

1	2	3
The remedy contains opium and eases the pain. You feel more relaxed lying down at home. Go to 16.	Purging. If you have a headache, the purging makes you feel weaker. Go to 24. If you have a pain in your side or you are vomiting, the purging makes you feel worse. Go to 22.	You wake up feeling better. The vomiting has stopped. Your stomach feels more settled. Go to 16.
4 Trephining. The doctor drills carefully into your skull. Was this a good idea? Toss a coin. Heads go to 12. Tails go to 23.	**5** The visit to the temple has relaxed you, but you need more rest. If you can afford time off work, then go for a walk, get some fresh air and go to 16. If not, choose another healer so that you can get back to work and earn some money quickly.	**6** If you are vomiting, the doctor offers you a herbal remedy. If you take it, go to 10. If not, go to 17. For a side-pain the doctor recommends rest and then exercise. If you agree, go to 14. If not, go to 17. For a headache the doctor suggests trephining. If you agree, go to 4. If not, go to 17.
7 Sadly you have just died.	**8** You wake up feeling even worse. Your arm is swollen where the blood was taken and you feel feverish. You feel sicker and sicker. Go to 7.	**9** You can only see this doctor if you are the senator or his wife. If you are, go to 6. If you are not, choose another healer.
10 Herbal remedy. If you have a side-pain the remedy has no effect. Go to 17. If you are vomiting, take the remedy, then go home and fall asleep. Go to 3.	**11** At the temple you get a good night's rest. You feel better but a few hours later the problem returns. If you have a headache, go to 5. If you are vomiting or have a side-pain, go to 17.	**12** The trephining seems to have worked. You feel better and the small hole gradually heals. Go to 16.
13 For a headache the doctor suggests trephining. If you agree, go to 4. If you do not, go to 17. For vomiting the doctor suggests bleeding or purging. If you decide on bleeding, go to 18. If purging, go to 2. If neither go to 17. For a side-pain the doctor suggests a herbal remedy. If you agree, go to 10. If not, go to 17.	**14** Rest, fresh air, exercise and a better diet. If you have a headache, you feel better after a few days. Go to 16. If you have a side-pain the treatment does not help. Go to 17.	**15** This quack remedy has weakened your body and made the problem worse. Go to 7.
16 The symptoms have disappeared and you have recovered.	**17** Either you do not like the treatment or the cure you chose has not worked. Choose again.	**18** Bleeding. This makes you feel weaker. Go home and sleep. Toss a coin. Heads go to 20. Tails go to 8.
19 At home you take a herbal remedy that your family has used for years. It contains honey, rhubarb and lots of other ingredients. Then lie down to sleep. If you have a headache, go to 1. If you are vomiting, go to 3. If you have a side-pain, go to 22.	**20** You wake feeling better. Perhaps rest was all that was needed. Go to 16.	**21** At the shop you buy Plautus' Remedy for All Ailments. Sounds good! It will certainly purge your bowels. Go to 2.
22 This wasn't the right treatment. It might have worked for another illness, but you feel worse – and worse. Go to 7.	**23** You feel better for a day but then a fever begins. Perhaps the instruments were not clean. Go to 7.	**24** The purging has made you feel weaker but at least it hasn't made the headache worse. You're still alive. Go to 17.

Would you survive in ancient Rome?

Use this worksheet to record your progress in the game on pages 50–51.

■ Who are you?

_____

■ What is wrong with you?

_____

■ Which healer have you chosen?

_____

	Square	Treatment	Result
1.			
2.			
3.			
4.			
5.			

■ Did you survive?

_____

From prehistory to the Romans: how much change?

Use this worksheet to complete the Task on page 52.

	Prehistory	Egypt	Greece	Rome
Medical problems	Pain, infection, disease, bleeding	Pain, infection, disease, bleeding	Pain, infection, disease, bleeding	Pain, bleeding. Infection and disease became greater problems
Who treated illnesses?	Medicine men, family, particularly women		Trained doctors, priests at Asclepeia, women in families	Trained doctors, priests at temples, women in families
What did they think caused illnesses?		Gods. Another explanation was that food rotting in the body caused disease	Gods, the humours in the body becoming unbalanced	Some believed in gods. The humours in the body becoming unbalanced
How did they prevent and treat illness?	Herbal remedies, charms, setting broken bones	Herbal remedies, simple surgery, charms		Herbs, simple operations, treatment by opposites, advice on exercise, public health schemes
Was life expectancy improving?	Nearly everyone died before the age of 40	Some of the wealthy probably lived a little longer	Some of the wealthy lived into their 60s	

Did women play a more important role than men in the early history of medicine?

Use this worksheet to help answer Task 2A on page 53. Use these questions as the basis for each paragraph of your essay.

■ What roles did men play as healers?
(medicine men; trained doctors; teachers and writers of medical books)

_____

_____

_____

_____

_____

_____

_____

■ What roles did women play in the home?
(treating everyday illnesses; using herbs)

_____

_____

_____

_____

_____

_____

_____

■ What roles did women play outside the home?
(as midwives; as doctors)

_____

_____

_____

_____

_____

_____

_____

■ Did men or women have a more important role?
(numbers of people treated; everyday importance; importance for future developments)

_____

_____

_____

_____

_____

_____

_____

Did ancient healers and medicines help the sick?

Use this worksheet to help answer Task 2B on page 53. Use these questions as the basis for each paragraph of your essay.

- What kinds of healers were there?
  (medicine men; doctors; women)

  _____

  _____

  _____

  _____

  _____

- What kinds of everyday treatments were used and did they work?
  (herbal remedies; healing broken bones and cuts; charms)

  _____

  _____

  _____

  _____

  _____

- What treatments and advice did doctors use and did they work?
  (bleeding, treatment of opposites; diet and exercise; simple surgery)

  _____

  _____

  _____

  _____

  _____

- Did priests and medicine men help the sick?
  (charms and spells; visits to Asclepeia)

  _____

  _____

  _____

  _____

  _____

- Did ancient healers help the sick?
  (low life expectancy; problem of epidemic diseases; success of some everyday treatments)

  _____

  _____

  _____

  _____

  _____

Hippocrates and Galen

Use this worksheet with the Activity on page 54. It will help you gather together the information for your obituary.

	Hippocrates	Galen
Significant dates	Born 460BC	2nd century AD
Where he lived and worked		
Claims to fame	■ dissection ■ observation ■ written works	■ observation ■ theory of the four humours ■ written works
Other information		

Medicine & Health Through Time

Did health decline in the Middle Ages? A case study of York

Use this worksheet to complete the Task on page 61. Use each sentence to begin a paragraph. Then use the answers to the questions in brackets to complete each paragraph.

■ York makes a good case study because there is plenty of evidence about people's health. (What kinds of evidence are there from York? What other kinds of evidence tell us about health in the Middle Ages?)

_____

_____

_____

_____

_____

■ After the Romans left Britain, the health of the people of York probably became worse. (How had the Romans protected health? How long did Anglo-Saxons live? What did they suffer from? What were their living conditions like?)

_____

_____

_____

_____

_____

■ Viking York was a very unhealthy city. (Why did disease spread easily? What did people suffer from?)

_____

_____

_____

_____

_____

■ Conditions in York became healthier in the later Middle Ages. (How were houses and diets changing? Was the city cleaner? How long did people live?)

_____

_____

_____

_____

_____

■ Now write your own conclusion to the essay!

_____

_____

_____

_____

_____

What did they think caused the Black Death?

Use this worksheet for the Activity on page 64.

What caused the Black Death?

A. **Common-sense reasons**

That privy stinks – smells like that make you ill!

B. **The body's humours are out of balance**

C. **The movement of the sun and the planets**

E. **Invisible fumes or poisons in the air**

D. **God and the Devil**

Something attacked me but I couldn't see what it was . . . and it's attacked you too!

What did they do about public health in fourteenth-century London?

Use this worksheet for the Activity on page 67.

Mark on the picture the fourteen scenes listed in the Students' Book.

Did people care about public health in fourteenth-century London?

1. What can you learn about life in London from Sources A and B?

_____

_____

2. Read Source C. Did people care about dirt and hygiene in London in the 1300s?

_____

_____

3. Why did the number of complaints in Source D rise and fall in the 1300s?

_____

_____

4. Did Londoners in the 1300s think that disease was linked to dirt? Explain your answer using these sources and pages 66–67 of your textbook.

_____

_____

_____

SOURCE A Barbara Hanawalt, *Growing Up in Medieval London*, 1993. Richard Whittington was Lord Mayor of London

66 *Richard Whittington, of storybook fame, left money [in his will] for a latrine that provided two rows of 64 seats each, one for men and one for women. The latrines were located where they would be flushed out by the tide.* 99

SOURCE B From the records of the City of London

66 *1326: Richard the Baker drowned when he used a public privy. As he sat down the rotten floorboards gave way. He fell into the cesspit beneath and drowned.* 99

SOURCE C From the records of the City of London

66 *1326: a pedlar in Cheap Street threw eel skins into the lane between two shops. Apprentices from the shops attacked the pedlar and killed him. [Anyone convicted of littering the streets was usually fined 4d – fourpence.]* 99

SOURCE D From the records of the City of London

Number of complaints about butchers' waste in the streets:

- 1300–1350   2
- 1350–1400   21
- 1400–1450   3
- 1450–1500   4

Number of entries in London records about street cleaning:

- 1300–1350   16
- 1350–1400   65
- 1400–1450   24
- 1450–1500   9

Medicine & Health Through Time

Did medieval hospitals help the sick?

Use this worksheet to complete the Activity on page 73.

Was there more continuity than change in the Middle Ages?

Use this worksheet to answer question 1 on page 80. Fill in the second row using the information in your textbook.

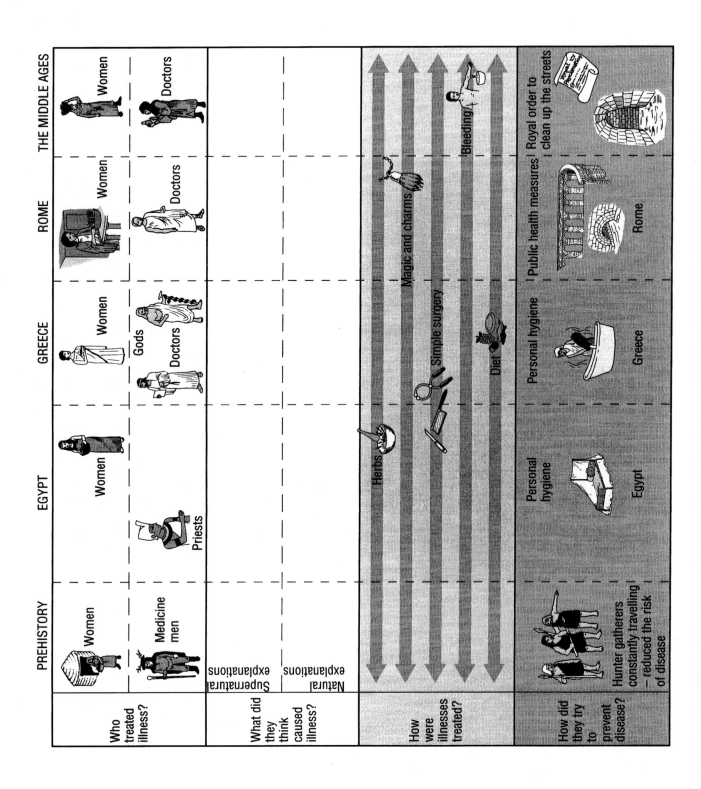

Paré and the bezoar stone

Read the Source below and answer questions 1–5.

1. What did people believe about the bezoar stone before Paré's experiment?

_____

_____

2. How did Paré test the effectiveness of the bezoar stone?

_____

_____

3. What did Paré's experiment prove?

_____

_____

4. What evidence is there in the Source that Galen's ideas were still used?

_____

_____

5. In what way is Paré's work a sign of new attitudes in science and medicine?

_____

_____

SOURCE From the *Apology and Treatise* of Ambroise Paré

66 *In Persia there is a kind of goat in whose stomach grows the stone called bezoar. This stone resembles an acorn. It is dark green. It is not very hard so that it can easily be scraped or dissolved in water.*

Some years ago a certain gentleman, who had one of these stones, bragged before King Charles [of France] about how effective this stone was against all poisons. Then the King asked me whether there was any antidote that was equally good against all poisons. I answered that all poisons do not have the same effects nor do they have the same cause. Therefore each must have its own proper and contrary antidote, as to the hot, that which is cold . . .

It was an easy matter to try out the stone on those condemned to be hanged. This plan pleased the King. A cook who was to be hanged for stealing two silver dishes from his master's house was brought by the jailor. The King asked whether he would take the poison, on condition that if the stone saved him from death then he should have his life. The cook answered cheerfully that he was willing to undergo the hazard. He took the poison and then some of the bezoar. A while after he began to vomit and to cry out that his inward parts were burnt with fire. Desiring water, they gave it to him.

An hour later, I found him on the ground like a beast upon hands and feet, with his tongue thrust out of his mouth, his eyes fiery, vomiting and blood flowing forth by his ears, nose and mouth. I gave him eight ounces of oil to drink but it did him no good.

At last he died with great torment, seven hours after he took the poison. I opened the body in the presence of the jailor and four others and found the bottom of his stomach black and dry as if it had been burnt by a cautery. The bezoar had failed to stop the poison. Therefore the King commanded that the bezoar be burned. 99

What caused the discoveries of the Medical Renaissance?

Use this worksheet to answer the questions on page 90.

EXPERIMENT
People were willing to challenge old ideas – by experimenting they could prove whether their theories were correct.

CHALLENGES
Many old ideas were challenged. Copernicus said the earth travelled round the sun, not the sun round the earth. Protestants challenged the Pope and the Catholic church.

WARS
There were many wars in 16th- and 17th-century Europe.

WEALTH
Since the Black Death in the 1300s many people had grown wealthier. They had money to spend on luxuries and education.

EDUCATION
Literacy was increasing and there were many more schools in the 16th and 17th centuries.

MACHINERY
There were improvements in clocks, watches, pumps and other machines.

ART
Skilful artists found work and people to buy their sculptures and paintings.

ANCIENT LEARNING
There was renewed interest in the writings of Roman and Greek thinkers.

PRINTING
From the late 1400s printed books meant that new ideas spread much more rapidly.

Did the Medical Renaissance improve health and treatments?

Use this worksheet to complete the Activity on page 92.

	Grace Mildmay	Richard Wiseman	Treating the plague 1665	James Woodforde
Old ideas				
New ideas from:				
■ Vesalius				
■ Paré				
■ Harvey				
■ Others?				

The health jigsaw in 1700

Use this worksheet to answer question 2 on page 103. Use these sentences to begin your paragraphs.

■ The doctor in 1700 still had some things in common with Galen and medieval doctors but he also knew more about the body.
(treatments, including herbs and bleeding; understanding of the cause of disease; new knowledge of anatomy and physiology)

_____

_____

_____

_____

_____

_____

_____

_____

_____

■ The doctor in 1700 had a little in common with doctors of today.
(improving knowledge of anatomy and physiology in the 1600s; treatments; but no understanding of the cause of disease in 1700; simpler equipment in 1700)

_____

_____

_____

_____

_____

_____

_____

_____

_____

■ Now choose one of these sentences to begin your conclusion:
 – A doctor in 1700 had more in common with earlier doctors than with doctors today.
 – A doctor in 1700 had more in common with doctors today than with earlier doctors.

_____

_____

_____

_____

_____

_____

_____

_____

How would you treat Charles II?

Use this worksheet to record the way you treated Charles II. You can choose as many of the options for each decision as you like. After you have made your choices work out your score from page 110.

Decisions – tick your choice	Reasons for your choices	Score

1   a) open a vein
      b) Mistress Holder
      c) nothing
      d) X-ray		

2   a) bleed
      b) nothing
      c) purge
      d) pray		

3   a) purge
      b) shout at servants
      c) pigeons
      d) shave head		

4   a) Mistress Holder
      b) bleed
      c) purge
      d) run away		

5   a) bleed
      b) purge
      c) use medicine
      d) abandon treatments		

6 yes no		

7   a) send your bill
      b) see James II
      c) run away		

Medicine from prehistory to 1700: a summary

Use this worksheet to complete Task 1 on page 108. Fill in the final column with a description of the main developments since 1400.

	PREHISTORY	EGYPT	GREECE	ROME	THE MIDDLE AGES	1400–1750
Who treated illness?	Women / Medicine men	Women / Priests	Women / Doctors / Gods	Women / Doctors	Women / Doctors	
What did they think caused illness? (Supernatural explanations)		Spirits and gods		Spirits and gods	Spirits, gods and planets	
What did they think caused illness? (Natural explanations)		The channels of your body are blocked	The four humours are out of balance	The four humours are out of balance	The four humours are out of balance	
How were illnesses treated?		Herbs / Simple surgery	Diet	Magic and charms	Bleeding	
How did they try to prevent disease?	Hunter gatherers constantly travelling – reduced the risk of disease	Personal hygiene / Egypt	Personal hygiene / Greece	Public health measures / Rome	Public health measures	

Was the Medical Renaissance an important period in medical history?

Use this worksheet to complete Task 4 on page 109.

Use these sentences as the openings to the paragraphs of your essay.

■ This was an important period because of discoveries about anatomy.

_____

_____

_____

_____

■ There were also important discoveries about the way the body worked.

_____

_____

_____

_____

■ This was also a time when surgeons began to use some more successful methods.

_____

_____

_____

_____

_____

■ However, most treatments remained the same as they had done for centuries.

_____

_____

_____

_____

■ Despite the new discoveries doctors still did not understand what caused disease.

_____

_____

_____

_____

■ By 1700 people could not expect to live longer than they had done centuries earlier.

_____

_____

_____

_____

■ Now choose one of these sentences to begin your conclusion:
  - The period between 1400 and 1750 was important because of the increase in knowledge of anatomy and physiology.
  - The period between 1400 and 1750 was not very important because the discoveries did not improve people's life expectancy.

_____

_____

_____

How did changes in the nineteenth century affect medicine and health?

Use this worksheet to record information about how changes in the nineteenth century affected medicine and health.

Changes during the nineteenth century	Effects on medicine and health
Urbanisation The growth of towns created many health problems. Poor housing and infected water supplies made killer diseases spread more rapidly than ever before.	
Technology New technology helped medicine. For example, developments in steelmaking helped to produce a thin syringe needle that did not break; improvements in glass-making led to better microscopes and the first thermometer.	
Scientific medicine Science helped medicine. Scientists discovered the links between micro-organisms and disease. Chemists researching the properties of different substances found, for example, a gas which could be used as an anaesthetic and a dye which killed bacteria.	
Entrepreneurs Medicine became big business. Some entrepreneurs made millions of pounds from almost useless remedies. However, others put money into scientific research to find drugs which would help to cure disease.	
Political change In 1800 Parliament believed it should not interfere in people's lives. If people were unhealthy that was their business! By 1900 Parliament was making laws to improve people's health in a way that would have been unthinkable in earlier centuries: for example, forcing towns to install sewers.	

Improved communications
 Communications were revolutionised in this period.
   Faster trains allowed scientists and doctors to gather at conferences and learn from each other's ideas. By 1900 you could get from London to Edinburgh in nine hours and from London to Paris in less than a day.
   There were more newspapers because improved education meant more people could read. News could be reported more quickly because of the invention of the telegraph. For example, details of important scientific experiments carried out in France were reported in British newspapers the next day.	

War Major wars during the period affected developments in health. For example, the Crimean War in the nineteenth century led to improvements in the standards of nursing and hospitals.	

Living conditions in the nineteenth century

Use this worksheet as an introduction to Chapter 4. Read the source and then answer the questions.

> **SOURCE** A description of some aspects of the living conditions of a wealthy family living close to London in the 1850s and 1860s, written by the historian Anthony Wohl in his book *Endangered Lives*
>
> 66 *Despite its wealth the family found that it was unable to isolate itself from the stinks, pollution, and health hazards of the day. As newly-weds they had wanted the latest sanitary appliances, but the inexperience of the workmen putting in the water closet resulted in the waste overflowing into the rain pipe and down the dressing room window. The cesspools beneath their Thameside residence were notoriously foul, even by the standards of the day and when at last they had a drainage system installed, the stench from the old cesspools remained and made parts of the dwelling almost uninhabitable. Some twenty years later the sewers blocked up after the heavy rains and became 'most offensive and putrid'. Although living by the Thames was most scenic, whenever the river rose the lawns were saturated by raw sewage, which habitually floated on the surface of the water. Resigned to this inevitability, they simply had the lawns raked and the filth shovelled back into the river. In drier weather on the other hand, the Thames muck was left high and dry along the banks and gave off an appalling odour.*
>
> *Probably as a consequence of the poor drainage, the father contracted one of the 'filth diseases' – bowel fever or typhoid – and after struggling through a crisis on Friday, 13 December, succumbed the following day. The mother had contracted typhoid herself when she was sixteen and quite understandably she dreaded the disease which was a major killer. She was also morbidly superstitious, so one can imagine her horror when her eldest son came down with typhoid and reached a crisis also on 13 December, exactly ten years after the father's. But to her immense relief and amazement, her son pulled through and was miraculously snatched back from, as she put it, 'the very verge of the grave ... hardly anyone had been known to recover who had been so ill as he was.' December 14, the day that had made her like so many others in that era, a young widow, always filled her with foreboding. Perhaps her superstitious dread was justified, for on that day one of her daughters, Alice, died of a disease, diphtheria, that was as puzzling as it was common (it also carried off her granddaughter). She no doubt consoled herself with the thought that compared to so many mothers she had been fortunate, for of her nine children not one had died in childbirth ... 99*

1. Complete this diagram to show the health problems faced by this family.

Sewage

Diseases

HEALTH PROBLEMS

Childbirth

2. Would you say that this family was more healthy or less healthy than most people living in London at this time?

_____

_____

Causes of death

Use this worksheet to help you answer questions 5 and 6 on page 114.

Remember in your answer that the stastistics are not comparing like with like. For example, Source 2 on page 114 specifies cause of death for only half the known deaths. Source 2 on page 170 gives national statistics. Source 2, on page 114, and Source 2 on page 102 are local.

Question 5

In the late seventeenth century the three main causes of death in Adel were _____ ,
_____ , _____ . Consumption or TB also caused _____ deaths.

Two hundred years later in Maidstone _____ was still a major problem, but _____ was not.

It is not clear from the Maidstone statistics whether _____ was still a problem in 1889, but my wider knowledge suggests it probably _____ .

_____

Question 6

Between 1889 and 1992 there was more/less change than between 1700 and 1889.

(Explain why) _____

_____

_____

_____

_____

_____

_____

_____

_____

_____

Two of the big killers from 1889 _____ , _____ have been almost eliminated.
_____ remains a problem however.

Comparing these statistics is difficult because _____

_____

_____

_____

_____

_____

_____

_____

_____

The killer diseases

Use this worksheet to complete the Activity on page 115.

Alongside each disease explain whether you think urbanisation would increase the risk of the disease spreading. You may find that your answers for many of the diseases are similar.

Disease	Did urbanisation contribute to the spread of the disease in the nineteenth century? Give reasons for your answer.
TB (Tuberculosis)	
Diphtheria	
Whooping cough	
Typhoid	
Bronchitis/pneumonia	
Influenza	
Cholera	
Smallpox	
Measles	

Two views of vaccination

'The Cowpock – or – the Wonderful Effects of the New Inoculation' by James Gillray, 1802

'The curse of humankind' by George Cruickshank, 1808

Murray's encyclopaedia

Use this worksheet to complete the Activity with Source 10 on page 119.

■ Jenner, Edward (1749–1823) English physician, discoverer of . . .

_____

_____

_____

> ### Additional Information
> – born in Berkeley, Gloucestershire
> – apprenticed to a surgeon at Salisbury
> – studied in London under John Hunter and then returned to Berkeley in 1773
> – began to investigate cowpox in 1775

■ Jenner was . . .

_____

_____

_____

■ Jenner developed vaccination . . .

_____

_____

_____

_____

_____

_____

_____

■ The work of Jenner was important . . .

_____

_____

_____

_____

_____

_____

_____

_____

_____

_____

A nineteenth-century statue of Jenner injecting the arm of James Phipps

Would your child survive in nineteenth-century Britain?

Use this worksheet to record your answers to question 7 of the Activity on page 120.

Mr and Mrs Grace are very well off. They inherited land and money from their parents.

Mr Gilbert is a clerk in a shipping office, working ten hours a day. He does not want his wife to work as that would not be 'respectable'. They have just enough money to live on, provided there are no unexpected bills.

Mrs Williams earns a few pennies doing laundry. Her husband works at the docks, provided an 'ill wind' does not keep the ships out of port. If there are no ships he earns nothing.

■ How helpful were the:

   1. Healers?

   _____
   _____
   _____

   2. Treatments?

   _____
   _____
   _____

   3. Remedies?

   _____
   _____
   _____

■ How helpful were the:

   1. Healers?

   _____
   _____
   _____

   2. Treatments?

   _____
   _____
   _____

   3. Remedies?

   _____
   _____
   _____

■ How helpful were the:

   1. Healers?

   _____
   _____
   _____

   2. Treatments?

   _____
   _____
   _____

   3. Remedies?

   _____
   _____
   _____

WILL YOUR CHILD SURVIVE?

1 Your choice of doctor depends on how much money you have. Graces go to 11. Gilberts go to 20. Williamses go to 27.	**2** Your sister says you must keep the child wrapped up warm at home with the window closed. If you agree, go to 14. If not, go to 7.	**3** Buy Morrison's Vegetable Universal Compound, pills that cure everything by purging the patient. Go to 14.	**4** At the herbalist the Williamses cannot afford the prices. Choose another healer. The Graces and Gilberts decide to try a herbal cure. The herbalist recommends treacle, tincture of lobelia and aniseed water. If you agree, go to 29.
5 The dispensary gives free medicine to working people who don't have much money. You try the medicine. Go to 25.	**6** The Williamses discover they cannot afford any more pills. Go to 22. The Graces and Gilberts buy some more. Go to 25.	**7** You are given lots of advice. If you listen to your friend, go to 26. If you listen to your sister, go to 2. If you listen to your brother, go to 18.	**8** The chemist mixes you a remedy made from sodium tartrate, Ipecacuhana wine and laudanum. The Williamses cannot afford this mixture. Choose another healer. If the Graces and Gilberts choose this remedy, go to 15. If they do not, choose another healer.
9 On your way home you meet a man selling Dr Drummond's Herbal Tonic which he says cures any disease or disability. If you buy some, go to 16. If not, choose another healer.	**10** There is still no improvement. The doctor suggests you take the child to the seaside to drink seawater. It can be very effective. If you agree, go to 19. If you disagree, go to 22.	**11** Your physician is very confident. He has seen plenty of these cases. He recommends bleeding the child, followed by purging. If you agree, go to 24. If not, choose another healer.	**12** The bleeding and purging bring no improvement. The doctor recommends another medicine to help your child vomit to clear out her system. You can't afford the medicine so he sends you to 5.
13 You take the child home, but you have no work so it is hard to feed her. Go to 17.	**14** The treatment has no immediate effect. You could try some more and go to 6 or, if not, go to 22.	**15** The remedy is not working. The chemist suggests doubling the dose. The Gilberts cannot afford more. Choose another healer. The Graces can afford another dose. If you choose this, go to 23. If not, choose another healer.	**16** Dr Drummond's Herbal Tonic cures almost everything but not your child's fever. Choose another healer.
17 The doctor says the child is no better. He says he will try bleeding her, but he is not hopeful. Go to 30.	**18** Your brother says the best remedy is to skin and roast a mouse and then get the child to eat it whole. If you agree, go to 28. If not, go back to 7.	**19** The journey is too much for the weak child. She dies. When the physician's bill arrives you pay it. He did everything he could.	**20** Your doctor recommends bleeding the child and then regular doses of purging. If you agree, go to 12. If you disagree, go to 22.
21 At the shop there are many patent medicines to choose from. Choose 3 or 31.	**22** It is time to choose another healer or go to 9.	**23** Your child recovers. Perhaps there was something in the remedy or perhaps it was because your child had clean bedding, plenty of food and fresh water.	**24** The bleeding and purging have not helped. Your doctor bleeds the child again and also makes her vomit. Go to 10.
25 There is still no improvement. Choose another healer or go to 30.	**26** Your friend says that the best remedy is for the child to ride a donkey seven times in a circle or be passed under it seven times. If you agree, go to 14. If not, go back to 7 or choose another healer.	**27** The doctor for the poor thinks it is best to bleed the child but says she is too weak through lack of food. He recommends you take her home to rest and to feed her and then bring her back. If you agree, go to 13. If not, choose another healer.	**28** Your child dies. Your brother says there was nothing wrong with his suggestion. You should have listened to him sooner.
29 The fever falls briefly then returns. If you decide to go back to the herbalist, go to 32. If not, choose another healer.	**30** Your child grows weaker and dies. You do not blame the doctor or the medicines. They were the best you could get.	**31** Buy Holloway's pills and ointment which cure everything by purging the patient. Go to 14.	**32** The herbalist recommends a mixture of dropwort and comfrey. The Gilberts cannot afford another treatment and choose another healer. The Graces buy the mixture and go to 23.

Women fight to become doctors

Use this worksheet for the Activity on page 124.

Photocopy and cut out each panel to pair up the boxes.

Box A

During the 1860s Elizabeth Garrett worked as a nurse and then attended lectures at the Middlesex Hospital.

Box B

Elizabeth Garrett passed all the exams to qualify as a doctor. The final step before she could work as a doctor was to become a member of one of the Colleges of Surgeons, Physicians or Apothecaries.

Box C

In 1874 six women, led by Sophia Jex-Blake, completed the medical course at Edinburgh University.

Box D

In 1876 a law was passed opening all medical qualifications to women.

Box E

The Colleges of Surgeons and Physicians refused to allow women members which therefore stopped Elizabeth from working as a doctor. She had to take the College of Apothecaries to court before it accepted her as a member. After that it too changed its rules so that women could not become members.

Box G

For five years after 1876 the Royal College of Surgeons refused to allow anyone to take exams in midwifery as a way of preventing women learning alongside men.

Box F

Male students at the hospital protested that Elizabeth Garrett should not be allowed to attend lectures.

Box H

Edinburgh University said that it could only give medical degrees to men. The women had to complete their degrees at Dublin or Zurich in Switzerland.

Factors affecting women's roles in medicine

Use this worksheet to answer question 5 on page 125 and the three questions below.

1. Using coloured pencils circle the factors that helped limit the role of women in medicine in one colour and those factors that helped increase the role of women in another.
2. Draw a line between each of the factors that are listed.
3. What were the most important factors in limiting the role of women in medicine?

_____

_____

_____

Government

Technology

Education

Religion

Individuals

Mary Seacole

Mary Seacole (1805–81) was a Jamaican 'doctress' and businesswoman who became a celebrated figure in Britain because of her work during the Crimean War. She wrote her life story in *The Wonderful Adventures of Mrs Seacole in Many Lands* (1857) which has since been republished by Falling Wall Press (1984). The sources in this worksheet are all from her autobiography.

■ TASK

Read through Sources 1–6, look at Source 7, and make notes in your own exercise book under the following headings:

1. How Mary Seacole learned her medical skills
2. What kind of treatments she used
3. What barriers she had to overcome to practise her medical skills
4. How her work was similar to/different from Florence Nightingale's.

SOURCE 1 Mary Seacole's childhood in Kingston, Jamaica

66 *My mother kept a boarding-house in Kingston, and was, like many of the Creole [mixed race] women, an admirable doctress; in high repute with the officers of both services, [navy and army] and their wives, who were from time to time stationed at Kingston. It was very natural that I should inherit her tastes ...*

... the ambition to become a doctress early took firm root in my mind; and I was very young when I began to make use of the little knowledge I had acquired from watching my mother, upon a great sufferer – my doll ...

Before long it was very natural that I should seek to extend my practice; and so I found other patients in the dogs and cats around me. Many luckless brutes had forced down their reluctant throats the remedies which I deemed most likely to suit their supposed complaints. And after a time I rose still higher in my ambition; and despairing of finding another human patient, I proceeded to try my remedies upon – myself.

When I was about twelve years old I was more frequently at my mother's house, and used to assist her in her duties; very often sharing with her the task of attending upon invalid officers or their wives, who came to her house from the adjacent camp at Up-Park, or the military station at Newcastle. 99

SOURCE 2 Aged 38, already widowed, Mary rebuilt her mother's hotel which had been destroyed by fire

66 *I had gained a reputation as a skilful nurse and doctress, and my house was always full of invalid officers and their wives from Newcastle, or the adjacent Up-Park Camp. Sometimes I had a naval or military surgeon under my roof, from whom I never failed to glean instruction, given, when they learned my love for their profession, with a readiness and kindness I am never likely to forget ...*

And here I may take the opportunity of explaining that it was from a confidence in my own powers, and not at all from necessity, that I remained an unprotected female. Indeed, I do not mind confessing to my reader, in a friendly confidential way, that one of the hardest struggles of my life in Kingston was to resist the pressing candidates for the late Mr. Seacole's shoes ...

While the cholera raged, I had but too many opportunities of watching its nature, and from a Dr. B–, who was then lodging in my house, received many hints as to its treatment which I afterwards found invaluable. 99

SOURCE 3 Aged 45, she travelled to mainland central America (modern-day Panama) to set up a hotel in Cruces

66 *I was not long in Cruces before my medicinal skill and knowledge were put to the test [when cholera struck]...*

There was no doctor in Cruces; the nearest approach to one was a little timid dentist, who was there by accident, and who refused to prescribe for the sufferer, and I was obliged to do my best. Selecting from my medicine chest – I never travel anywhere without it – what I deemed necessary, I went hastily to the patient, and at once adopted the remedies I considered fit. It was a very obstinate case, but by dint of mustard emetics [medicine that causes vomiting], warm fomentations, mustard plasters on the stomach and the back, and calomel [a purgative medicine], at first in large then in gradually smaller doses, I succeeded in saving my first cholera patient in Cruces.

... I sat before the flickering fire, with my [latest] patient in my lap – a poor, little, brown-faced orphan infant, scarce a year old, dead in my arms...

Then it was that I began to think – how the idea first arose in my mind I can hardly say – that, if it were possible to take this little child and examine it, I should learn more of the terrible disease which was sparing neither young nor old, and should know better how to do battle with it. I was not afraid to use my baby patient thus. I knew its fled spirit would not reproach me, for I had done all I could for it in life – had shed tears over it, and prayed for it...

This was my first and last post mortem examination. It seems a strange deed to accomplish, and I am sure I could not wield the scalpel or the substitute I then used now, but at that time the excitement had strung my mind up to a high pitch of courage and determination; and perhaps the daily, almost hourly, scenes of death had made me somewhat callous...

We buried the poor little body beneath a piece of luxuriant turf, and stole back into Cruces like guilty things. But the knowledge I had obtained thus strangely was very valuable to me, and was soon put into practice...

When my patients felt thirsty, I would give them water in which cinnamon had been boiled. One stubborn attack succumbed to an additional dose of ten grains of sugar of lead, mixed in a pint of water, given in doses of a tablespoonful every quarter of an hour. Another patient, a girl, I rubbed over with warm oil, camphor, and spirits of wine. Above all, I never neglected to apply mustard poultices to the stomach, spine, and neck, and particularly to keep my patient warm about the region of the heart. Nor did I relax my care when the disease had passed by, for danger did not cease when the great foe was beaten off. The patient was left prostrate; strengthening medicines had to be given cautiously, for fever, often of the brain, would follow. But, after all, one great conclusion, which my practice in cholera cases enabled me to come to was the old one, that few constitutions permitted the use of exactly similar remedies, and that the course of treatment which saved one man, would, if persisted in, have very likely killed his brother. 99

SOURCE 4 In 1854 when war broke out in the Crimea Mary Seacole came to London hoping to go as a nurse to serve the British army

66 *I made long and unwearied application at the War Office, in blissful ignorance of the labour and time I was throwing away... I grew tired at last and then I changed my plans.*

Now, I am not for a single instant going to blame the authorities who would not listen to the offer of a motherly yellow woman to go to the Crimea and nurse her 'sons' there, suffering from cholera, diarrhoea, and a host of lesser ills. In my country, where people know our use, it would have been different; but here it was natural enough – although I had references, and other voices spoke for me – that they should laugh, good-naturedly enough, at my offer. War, I know, is a serious game, but sometimes very humble actors are of great use in it...

My new scheme was, I candidly confess, worse devised than the one which had failed. Miss Nightingale had left England for the Crimea, but other nurses were still to follow, and my new plan was simply to offer myself as a recruit. Feeling that I was one of the very women they most wanted, experienced and fond of the work, I jumped at once to the conclusion that they would gladly enrol me in their number...

Many a long hour did I wait in this great hall, while scores passed in and out; many of them looking curiously at me. The flunkeys, noble creatures! marvelled exceedingly at the yellow woman whom no excuses could get rid of, nor impertinence dismay, and showed me very clearly that they resented my persisting in remaining there in mute appeal from their sovereign will...

At last I had an interview with one of Miss Nightingale's companions. She gave me the same reply, [that there were no vacancies], and I read in her face the fact, that had there been a vacancy, I should not have been chosen to fill it. 99

SOURCE 5 Rebuffed by the official bodies, she paid her own passage to the Crimea, went into partnership with a Mr Day setting up a hotel and store near the front line that sold food, drink and medical care to the soldiers. It was called the British Hotel

" I have never been long in any place before I have found my practical experience in the science of medicine useful ... In the Crimea, where the doctors were so overworked, and sickness was so prevalent, I could not be long idle; for I never forgot that my intention in seeking the army was to help the kind-hearted doctors, to be useful to whom I have ever looked upon and still regard as so high a privilege.

But before very long I found myself surrounded with patients of my own, and this for two simple reasons. In the first place, the men (I am speaking of the 'ranks' now) had a very serious objection to going into hospital for any but urgent reasons ... and, in the second place, they could and did get at my store sick-comforts and nourishing food, which the heads of the medical staff would sometimes find it difficult to procure. These reasons, with the additional one that I was very familiar with the diseases which they suffered most from and successful in their treatment (I say this in no spirit of vanity), were quite sufficient to account for the numbers who came daily to the British Hotel for medical treatment. "

SOURCE 6 Some of the testimonials to the work of Mary Seacole in the Crimea

" My dear Mrs. Seacole, – I have finished the bottle, which has done my jaundice a deal of good. Will you kindly send another by bearer. Truly yours, 'F.M.'

It was a capital prescription which had done his jaundice good. There was so great a demand for it, that I kept it mixed in a large pan, ready to ladle it out to the scores of applicants who came for it.

Sometimes they would send for other and no less important medicines. Here is such an application from a sick officer:-

'Mrs. Seacole would confer a favour on the writer, who is very ill, by giving his servant (the bearer) a boiled or roast fowl; if it be impossible to obtain them, some chicken broth would be very acceptable.

'I am yours, truly obliged, 'J.K., 18th R.S.'

Doesn't that read like a sick man's letter, glad enough to welcome any woman's face? Here are some gentlemen of the Commissariat anxious to speak for me:-

'Arthur C–, Comm. Staff Officer, having been attacked one evening with a very bad diarrhoea at Mrs. Seacole's, took some of her good medicine. It cured me before the next morning, and I have never been attacked since. – October 17th, 1855.'

Here is Mr. M–, paymaster of the Land Transport Corps, ready with a good account of my services:-

'I certify that Madame Seacole twice cured me effectually of dysentery while in the Crimea, and also my clerk and the men of my corps, to my certain knowledge.'

'Camp, near Karani, June 16, 1856
'My dear Mrs. Seacole, – As you are about to leave the Crimea, I avail myself of the only opportunity which may occur for some time, to acknowledge my gratitude to you ...

I am sure when her most gracious Majesty the Queen shall have become acquainted with the service you have gratuitously rendered to so many of her brave soldiers, her generous heart will thank you. For you have been an instrument in the hands of the Almighty to preserve many a gallant heart to the empire, to fight and win her battles, if ever again war may become a necessity. Please to accept this from your most grateful humble servant,
'W.J. Tynan.' "

SOURCE 7 Mary Seacole in the British Hotel

After the Crimean War Mary Seacole worked in both Jamaica and Britain. She died in London in 1881.

Germ theory and spontaneous generation

The diagrams on this worksheet may be useful for photocopying.

THEORY	EXPERIMENT	
The air contains living micro-organisms	He took sterile flasks out into the streets of Paris, opened them briefly, then sealed them again. Bacteria grew in them.	
Microbes are not evenly distributed in the air	He repeated the experiment in various places around France including high mountains. The number of bacteria varied.	
Microbes cause decay	He filled two flasks: one with sterile air and the other with ordinary air. In the first there was no decay; in the second decay proceeded as normal.	
Microbes can be killed by heating	He heated material in a flask to make it sterile. He drove the air out, then sealed the flask. It remained sterile even 100 years later.	

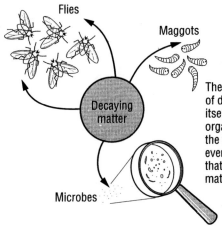

The old theory: Spontaneous generation

Flies

Maggots

Decaying matter

Microbes

The organisms are **the result** of decay. Decaying matter itself turns into living organisms. Early versions of the theory suggested that even the flies and maggots that were seen on decaying matter were created by it.

Germ theory

Flies lay eggs

Decaying matter

Eggs hatch into maggots

The living organisms fall from the air and **cause** decay.

Microbes in the air

The steps towards discovering the causes of disease

This worksheet can be used to help with the Task on page 129.

What the step involved	Why this step was so important	The important factors which helped scientists make the step
1		
2		
3		
4		
5		
6	Complete Step 6 after you have studied page 130.	

WORKSHEET 54

Robert Koch's work

Use this worksheet to annotate the drawing of Robert Koch and explain the main features of the cartoon.

Now try this.

1. What aspects of the work of Koch are not included in this cartoon?

____

____

____

____

____

2. Draw these aspects of his work on the cartoon and annotate them.

An interview with Robert Koch

Use this worksheet to answer question 1 on page 130.

■ My greatest achievement was . . .

_____
_____
_____
_____
_____
_____
_____
_____
_____

■ My research will help people in the future to . . .

_____
_____
_____
_____
_____
_____
_____
_____
_____
_____
_____

■ The most important factor in my success was . . .

_____
_____
_____
_____
_____
_____
_____
_____
_____
_____
_____

Why were Pasteur and Koch successful in solving the riddle of disease?

Use this worksheet for the Task on page 133.

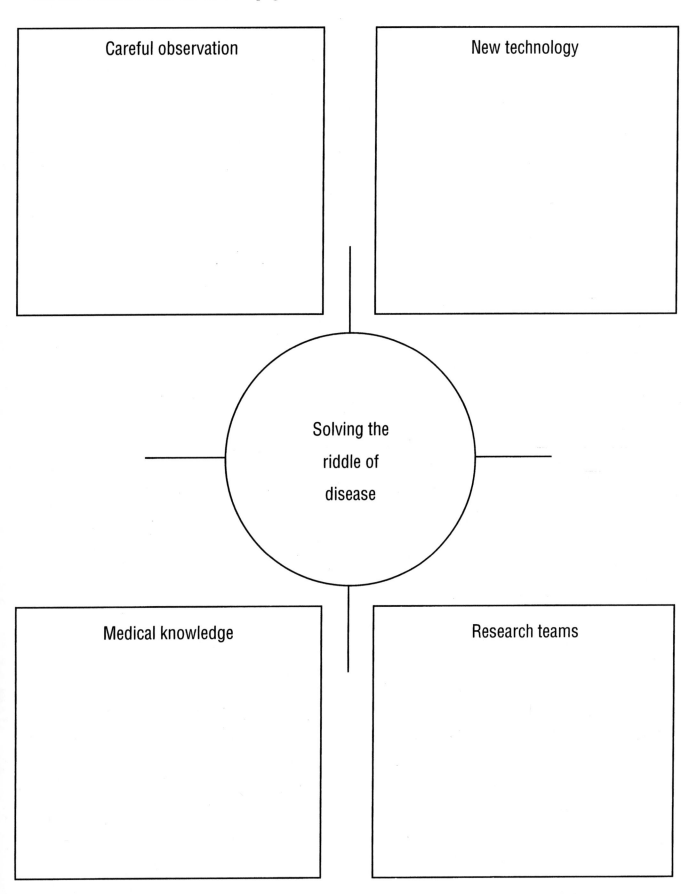

Careful observation

New technology

Solving the
riddle of
disease

Medical knowledge

Research teams

Why were the causes of disease finally discovered in the 1860s and 1870s?

Use this worksheet to help answer the essay in question 2 of the Task on page 133.

■ Before the 1860s scientists believed that the causes of disease were ...

_____

_____

_____

_____

_____

■ Careful observation was a characteristic of ...

_____

_____

_____

_____

_____

■ Increasing medical knowledge meant that the old theories ...

_____

_____

_____

_____

_____

■ For the first time it was clear that individuals needed to work in research teams. Pasteur ...

_____

_____

_____

_____

_____

■ The solving of the riddle of disease was due to ...

_____

_____

_____

_____

_____

■ The most important of these factors was ...

_____

_____

_____

_____

_____

How did scientists discover cures for disease?

Study Source 8 on page 133 and use this worksheet as a framework to explain how scientists discovered the first cures for disease.

■ The problem facing doctors in the middle of the nineteenth century was ...

_____

_____

_____

_____

■ Germ theory was developed by Louis Pasteur. He discovered that ...

_____

_____

_____

_____

■ In the 1860s Koch carefully studied many different bacteria. He ...

_____

_____

_____

_____

■ By the 1880s Pasteur had developed ...

_____

_____

_____

_____

■ Pasteur and Koch through their work were able to help prevent disease but they could not cure disease.

_____

_____

_____

_____

■ The first cures were developed by Behring and Ehrlich. Behring ...

_____

_____

_____

_____

■ Ehrlich began the real revolution in finding cures for diseases by producing a chemical compound that destroyed bacteria like a ...

_____

_____

_____

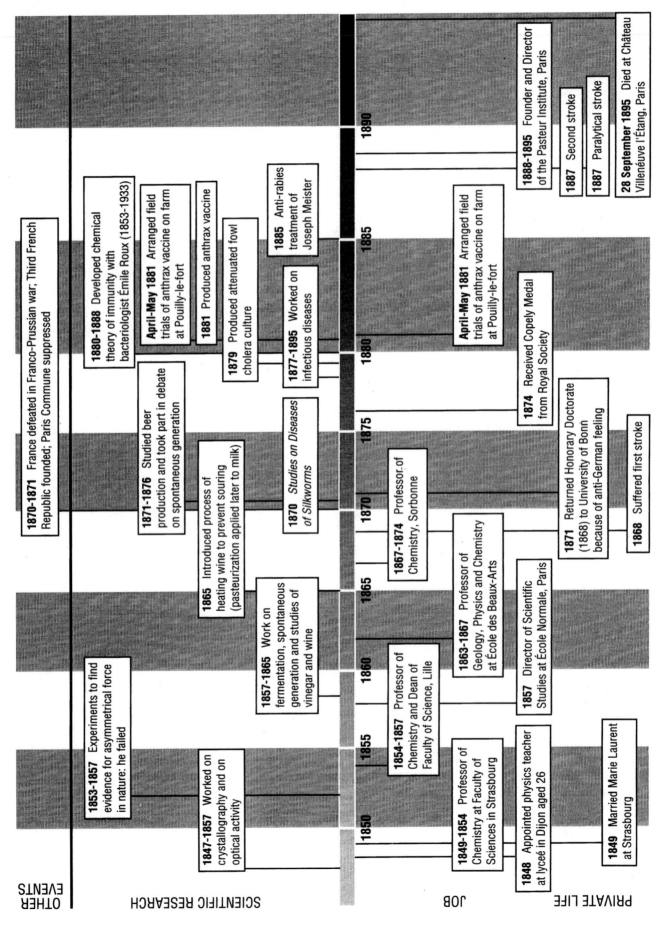

OTHER EVENTS

1870–1871 France defeated in Franco-Prussian war; Third French Republic founded; Paris Commune suppressed

SCIENTIFIC RESEARCH

1853–1857 Experiments to find evidence for asymmetrical force in nature: he failed

1847–1857 Worked on crystallography and on optical activity

1857–1865 Work on fermentation, spontaneous generation and studies of vinegar and wine

1865 Introduced process of heating wine to prevent souring (pasteurization applied later to milk)

1870 *Studies on Diseases of Silkworms*

1871–1876 Studied beer production and took part in debate on spontaneous generation

1880–1888 Developed chemical theory of immunity with bacteriologist Émile Roux (1853–1933)

April–May 1881 Arranged field trials of anthrax vaccine on farm at Pouilly-le-fort

1881 Produced anthrax vaccine

1879 Produced attenuated fowl cholera culture

1877–1895 Worked on infectious diseases

1885 Anti-rabies treatment of Joseph Meister

JOB

1849–1854 Professor of Chemistry at Faculty of Sciences in Strasbourg

1854–1857 Professor of Chemistry and Dean of Faculty of Science, Lille

1857 Director of Scientific Studies at École Normale, Paris

1863–1867 Professor of Geology, Physics and Chemistry at École des Beaux-Arts

1867–1874 Professor of Chemistry, Sorbonne

April–May 1881 Arranged field trials of anthrax vaccine on farm at Pouilly-le-fort

1874 Received Copely Medal from Royal Society

1888–1895 Founder and Director of the Pasteur Institute, Paris

PRIVATE LIFE

1848 Appointed physics teacher at lycée in Dijon aged 26

1849 Married Marie Laurent at Strasbourg

1868 Suffered first stroke

1871 Returned Honorary Doctorate (1868) to University of Bonn because of anti-German feeling

1887 Second stroke

1887 Paralytical stroke

28 September 1895 Died at Château Villenêuve l'Étang, Paris

1850 1855 1860 1865 1870 1875 1880 1885 1890

Why was surgery so dangerous in the early 1800s?

Use this worksheet with questions 1–3 on page 134.
Annotate the picture and explain:

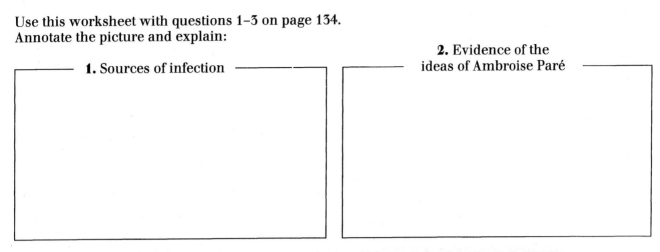

1. Sources of infection

2. Evidence of the ideas of Ambroise Paré

3. Why pain, bleeding and infection made surgery so dangerous.

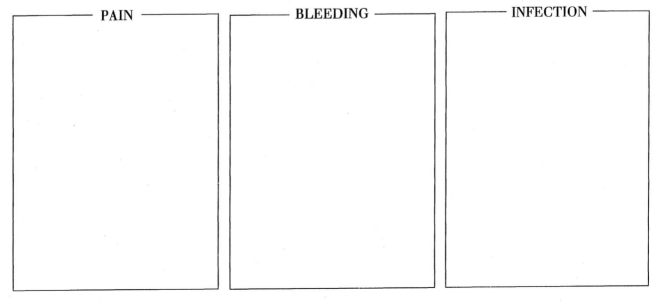

PAIN

BLEEDING

INFECTION

The development of anaesthetics

Use this worksheet for the Task on page 136.

Explain how all these factors played a role in either encouraging or opposing the development of anaesthetics.

Religion	War

Individual genius	Queen Victoria

Chance	Government

Opposition to Lister

Use this worksheet for the Activity on page 139.

OPPOSITION

Your notes

Some themes that may form the focus of your discussion:

The effects of carbolic spray

Time taken to operate with new methods

Difficulties in copying Lister's methods

Doubts about germ theory itself

Lister's personality

Lister changed his mind

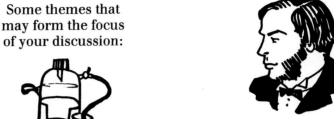

LISTER

Your notes

You may find it useful to research the arguments used by your opponents. This will help you understand and be able to undermine more effectively their opposition.

The link between Lister's work and germ theory

Use this worksheet for the Task on page 139.

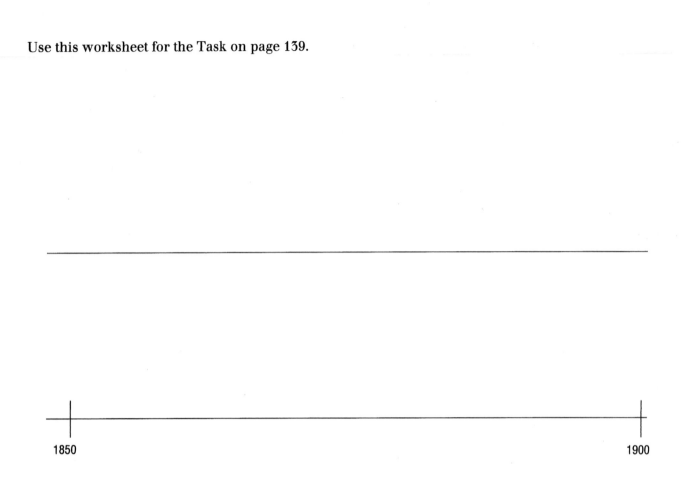

1850   1900

1. How was Lister's work linked to Pasteur's germ theory?

_____

_____

_____

_____

_____

2. What other factors helped lead to improvements in surgery?

_____

_____

_____

_____

Cholera!

Read the play on this worksheet before you start to look at the subject of cholera on page 140.

The scene is the small town of Krishnapur in India. It is the late summer of 1857. For several months the British residents of Krishnapur have been besieged by Indian rebels. Many have died in the attacks but the defenders have held out so far. Now a new and greater danger threatens to end the siege – cholera is spreading fast.

Cast of characters

MR SIMMONS	the governor of the town
MRS SIMMONS	his wife
DR DUNSTAPLE	the senior doctor, who has treated the people of Krishnapur for twenty years
LOUISE DUNSTAPLE	his daughter
DR McNAB	a young Scottish doctor, newly arrived
HARRY	a young officer, keen to keep up with new ideas
MIRIAM	Harry's sister
MRS JOHNSON	a middle-aged woman whose husband has been killed in the siege

Scene One

Outside the hospital ward. **Louise, Miriam** *and* **Mrs Johnson** *are helping out as nurses. They are snatching a breath of fresh air. Enter* **Harry**

HARRY   I don't know how you can work in that ward. The smell's awful.

MIRIAM   If you did work here you wouldn't notice the smell – there are worse things going on.

LOUISE   Yes, the flies are the biggest nuisance – they're everywhere. In your hair, on your face, inside your clothes . . .

MRS JOHNSON   And all over the food. We even have to spoon them out of the tea.

LOUISE   But the patients suffer more than we do – you're better off out on the battlements.

MRS JOHNSON   The vicar says the flies even get down his throat when he's saying prayers for the dying.

MIRIAM   Mind you, so many people are dying that he can't keep up any more – I don't think we can last much longer before we all get cholera.

HARRY   In that case I'll get back to the battlements – I'll feel safer.

Scene Two

Below the battlements. **Mr and Mrs Simmons** *are checking the defences.* **Harry** *rushes back from the hospital*

MR SIMMONS   It's all right, young man, there's no attack. They're having a rest out there – probably waiting for us to die off. How's the hospital?

HARRY   Pretty awful, sir. The doctors never seem to get any rest.

MRS SIMMONS   Not that they're saving anybody. They don't seem to be able to stop the cholera at all.

HARRY   I've got faith in McNab. He's a real scientist – he uses the latest methods and keeps his records. He'll find a cure.

MRS SIMMONS	But I don't want to be one of his records. They say he was making notes while his wife was dying. I'm not having that gloomy Scotsman looking after me if I get cholera. I've put a card in my pocket which says that only Dunstaple is to treat me.
MR SIMMONS	Dunstaple is far more experienced and he's always looked after us well. We trust him.
HARRY	Yes, he's very comforting – and very good at delivering babies – but he can't tackle cholera. I swear he's cracking up himself. McNab may be new and young, but I'm for him.
MRS SIMMONS	You're a fool, then. He'll be too busy experimenting to save you.

Scene Three

In the cellar below the Simmons's house. Prayers have just finished

DR DUNSTAPLE	Cholera! Ladies and gentlemen, we must discuss the danger. I don't need to tell you how serious the situation is. Many of our friends have died and more will do so. This is the will of God. But is it God's will that a man, I can't call him a doctor, should be helping people to their doom by using foolish treatments?
	We may not know how to stop cholera completely but doctors have a duty to use the best methods available. Doctors mustn't experiment or use fancy potions on their patients.
	(now shouting) I challenge Dr McNab to justify his methods, which go against all we know about the disease.
DR McNAB	I agree I use different methods from Dr Dunstaple. That's because we disagree about the cause of cholera. I believe that people catch cholera from the drinking water. Our water is infected by the waste from our sewers and so cholera is passed on from those who have the disease to those who have not.
DR DUNSTAPLE	Let me read you Dr Baly's conclusion, presented to the Royal College of Physicians in 1854. He says that the only theory supported by enough evidence is that cholera is caused by 'damp or impure air'.
MRS SIMMONS	There, I told you. The Royal College of Physicians ... McNab's a crackpot!
MIRIAM	Perhaps I'd better alter my card – I was worried about Dr Dunstaple, but if the Royal College agrees with him ...
MRS JOHNSON	There's so many crossings out on my card, I haven't got room to alter it again.
DR DUNSTAPLE	Do you remember the cholera epidemic in Newcastle in 1853? Everyone knows that for two months there was an invisible cholera cloud hanging over the town. Nearly everybody was affected by this bad air – yet people from outside the town were quite healthy. But if strangers came into Newcastle they quickly caught cholera and died. Bad air, ladies and gentlemen, that's the cause!
HARRY	But can you cure the disease? That's what we need, a cure!
DR DUNSTAPLE	I am using the normal treatment. Restore body heat with a warm bath and use other treatments which are opposite to the symptoms. We apply mustard plasters to the stomach, leeches to the head to cure headaches, a little brandy and opium tablets. That's the accepted treatment. Dr McNab only offers you his own experiments.
DR McNAB	It's quite untrue that there's one accepted treatment. The medical journals are full of different ideas, but no one seems sure. My treatment is based on the patient's symptoms too, but in a different way. The first sign of cholera is diarrhoea and the patient loses a lot of body liquid. I try to replace the lost fluid and body salts with injections. This doesn't weaken the patient even more, like Dr Dunstaple's methods.

DR DUNSTAPLE   Nonsense ...

He is interrupted by the sound of shooting – the rebels have renewed their attack

Scene Four
Several days later. Again following prayers

DR DUNSTAPLE   Ladies and gentlemen, for your sake, we must finish our debate with Dr McNab. He has explained why he uses his peculiar methods, which seem to amount to filling people full of water! I want to know one thing. Why does he think we get cholera from drinking water? We need proof, not fancy ideas.

DR McNAB   If you want a reason for my treatment, look at the patients. Inject a weak mixture of salt and water into a suffering patient and he changes before your eyes – he regains his colour and normal temperature, he's able to sit up and breathe properly. This wouldn't happen if cholera is caused by bad air affecting the lungs, as Dr Dunstaple tries to tell us.

LOUISE   It's true; I've seen it happen. It makes the patients stronger.

MIRIAM   Shh! Your father won't want you agreeing with McNab!

DR DUNSTAPLE   You still haven't told us how drinking water spreads cholera. How do you explain the fact that cholera is common in places known to have impure air?

DR McNAB   These places with 'impure air', as Dr Dunstaple calls it, are crowded by the poor, who have to live, cook, eat and sleep in the same room, with everyone packed together. In these conditions cholera gets passed on very easily. Doctors, priests and other visitors don't live in these conditions and they don't suffer from cholera so much.

DR DUNSTAPLE   But why drinking water, McNab?

DR McNAB   Let me give you just one example – the cholera outbreaks of 1849 and 1853–54. In 1849 south London was hit by cholera. Two water companies supplied the water but all districts were affected in the same way.
   Soon afterwards, one of the water companies moved its works. The Lambeth Company now gets its water from higher up the river, out of reach of London's sewage. When the 1853 epidemic broke out this saved thousands of people. Only 313 people who got their water from the Lambeth Company died of cholera – but over 2,400 died who got water from the Southwark and Vauxhall Company. Even if you remember that the Southwark and Vauxhall Company supplied twice as many houses, that's an amazing difference. And they supplied houses in the same streets, not in separate areas.
   This must prove to you that the water supply caused the spread of cholera.

DR DUNSTAPLE   I'll prove you wrong. Here's a bottle of your cholera-spreading water – I'll drink it, but I won't get cholera!

Scene Five
The next day

LOUISE   Miriam, Miriam, father's ill. He's vomiting and he's got diarrhoea – it must be the cholera!

MIRIAM   How are you treating him?

LOUISE   We're using his own methods. We have to! He keeps shouting 'Don't let McNab near me' and 'That Scottish fool mustn't try his tricks on me!'

MRS JOHNSON   Come quickly, Louise, it's your father – he's getting worse. I think he's unconscious.

LOUISE   I wish I knew what to do. Do you think I should get Dr McNab?

MIRIAM
You must, Louise. McNab's patients do get better – you said so yourself. Even your father can't complain if he gets better!

Scene Six
*Several hours later – by **Dr Dunstaple's** bed*

LOUISE
Miriam, he is getting better. Look, you can see his colour coming back . . . and his breathing's easier.

MIRIAM
It's a miracle. It was good of Dr McNab to treat him, after all your father's said about him.

DR DUNSTAPLE
(coming round)
Louise, is that you? I told you my methods would work . . . but where're the hot bandages? I don't remember having my pills . . . Have you let McNab see me? Are you trying to kill me, girl? You must use my methods!

LOUISE
All right, father, please calm down. I'll send for the pills and bandages. They'll soon have you back on your feet.

Scene Seven
*Three hours later – by **Dr Dunstaple's** bed*

LOUISE
I can't stand it. He's looking worse again. As soon as we gave him one of his pills and put the hot bandages on he got worse. What can I do?

DR McNAB
I'll treat him once more, but if he disobeys me, it'll be the end of him. Every time I revive him, he insults me.

DR DUNSTAPLE
(rambling)
I won't have that Scottish fake near me. You've let me down, Louise . . . everyone out of the room . . . I want Mrs Johnson to treat me . . . must use my own cures . . . I'll be better soon.

Scene Eight
The next day

HARRY
I'm sorry, Dr Dunstaple's dead. McNab's been right all along. If only the old doctor had listened to him.

MR SIMMONS
Nonsense, man. Who's to say that McNab's treatment works? Dunstaple died after all. Perhaps Dunstaple's methods were working until McNab interfered. These new ideas still haven't convinced me.

THE END

"A Court for King Cholera"

Add annotations to this cartoon to answer questions 1 and 2 on page 140.

Contemporary explanations of cholera: continuity or change?

Use this worksheet to answer questions 1–3 on page 141.

1.

What people believed caused the Black Death in the 1300s	Was it used as an explanation of cholera?	Evidence
A punishment from God		
Movements of the planets		
Earthquakes		
Children's misbehaviour		
Dirt in the streets		
Poisons in the air		

2. Other explanations

_____

_____

_____

_____

_____

3. Why were some medieval explanations for disease still being used?

_____

_____

_____

_____

_____

Were conditions the same in both rural and urban areas?

These cartoons from *Punch* illustrate that problems of ill health were to be found in both town and country areas.

1. Mark the common problems in the box between the cartoons. If there are problems particular to one area only annotate the cartoon.

───Common problems───

The Cottage
Mr. Punch (to Landlord). "Your stable arrangements are excellent!
Suppose you try something of the sort here! Eh?"
(Punch Almanac, 1861)

2. Do you think it is true to say that country areas were so much more healthy than the towns in the nineteenth century?

_____

_____

Medicine & Health Through Time

Why was public health finally improved? (i)

1. On this copy of Source 21 from page 146, draw arrows to show how these different causes are connected to each other.
2. Add other causes if you think there are some we have missed out. Show how they are connected too.

Scientific developments

Pasteur's germ theory had finally proved the link between dirt and disease.

Statistics

From 1837 the government collected statistics on births, marriages and deaths. William Farr used these to compile an accurate picture of where the death rate was highest and what people died of. He was able to prove, beyond any shadow of a doubt, a link between unhealthy living conditions and high death rates. He also published details of which were the most unhealthy towns which shamed some of them into action.

Cholera

In 1865 cholera came back again. With the link between the disease and dirty water proved once and for all by John Snow, and then explained by Pasteur's germ theory, ratepayers were finally prepared to take action to clean up their towns.

New voters

In 1867 working-class men had been given the vote. This meant that MPs were more likely to take notice of the people in their towns who were the main victims of poor public health.

These men can vote now so we must offer them something.

The 1875 Public Health Act

This laid down in detail all the duties that were expected of a local council. All towns were forced to perform these tasks. They included the provision of clean water, proper drainage and sewage, and the appointment of a Medical Officer of Health.

HM REGISTRY OF BIRTHS DEATHS & MARRIAGES

The weakening of *laissez-faire*

As a result of all these changes the government saw it could no longer leave important public health measures to individuals or councils. The government realised that it was in everyone's interest to force towns to clean up.

We can't tackle the problems on our own.

Education

Education was improving. In 1870 the government made every local authority set up schools.

Some cities led the way

Look at Leeds – a major industrial town – for example. Until 1866 very little action had been taken (see Source 18). Then in 1866 the town appointed its first Medical Officer of Health. In the same year a pressure group was formed to force the council to act. It was backed by the local newspaper who publicly blamed the council for 2,000 unnecessary deaths in Leeds each year. In 1870 a local firm got a court order to prevent sewage being pumped into the river from which it drew its own water. In 1874 Leeds had its first sewage purification works. In other towns, throughout the country, similar changes were taking place, and towns began to compete with each other to be the cleanest.

We will provide clean water and proper drainage and sewage systems.

Why was public health finally improved? (ii)

Our first task is to identify the different factors/causes.

Then we must see how these factors worked

Finally we try to work out which factor or factors were the most important reasons for

It was impossible to make any real improvements in public health in Britain before 1861. Discuss.

This worksheet will help you answer question 3 of the Task on page 146. Use the sentences below as the basis for each paragraph of your essay.

■ There had been some action taken when the cholera epidemic swept Britain ...

_____

_____

_____

_____

_____

■ In the years before 1861 it was very difficult for local government to provide public health facilities. Most town councils ...

_____

_____

_____

_____

_____

■ Until later in the century scientists did not really understand the causes of infectious disease. This meant that ...

_____

_____

_____

_____

_____

■ Ordinary people had very little understanding of the importance of basic hygiene with the result that ...

_____

_____

_____

_____

_____

■ It was very difficult for councils to make any real improvements in public health for a number of important reasons. The most significant of these are ...

_____

_____

_____

_____

Public health: research activity

Working in groups, research one or more of the items shown in Source 22 on page 147. You might also want to research other topics which we have not included.

Then on your own copy of Source 22 add notes to explain when, how and why each of these measures was introduced, and why they had an impact on health, in the same way that we have done for education.

Key date/s	How were these measures introduced?	Why were they introduced?	What impact did they have on health?
Improved education: 1870 onwards From 1870 every local authority had to set up schools.	The measures were introduced by parliament and involved areas establishing their own school boards.	There had been great debate about what sort of education system there should be, and how religion should be taught. By 1870 religious interests compromised and board schools were established.	Health education was taught at many schools. Improved literacy made it possible for people to read pamphlets from Medical Officers giving advice about drainage, ventilation, diet, personal cleanliness, care of children and care of the sick.
1802 onwards Factory Acts improved people's working conditions			
1876 Building regulations			
1889 Isolation hospitals for infectious diseases			
1852 Compulsory vaccination			
1858 Regulation of doctors' qualifications			
1876 Laws against pollution of rivers **1876** Food regulations improve the quality of food sold in shops			

A century of medical progress?

Use this worksheet for the Task on page 148.

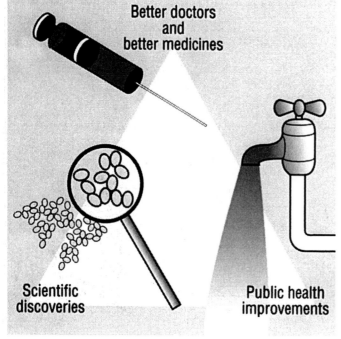

Better doctors and better medicines

Scientific discoveries

Public health improvements

Medicine & Health Through Time

A century of medical progress

Work in different groups to tackle each of the hypotheses A, B and C below.
1. Choose what you think is the most important point 'for' and 'against' your given hypothesis.
2. For each of the points you have selected find evidence from your textbook to support your argument.
3. Now use your research in a class debate: 'Public health reforms were more important than science or doctors in improving people's health in the nineteenth century.'
4. Using this worksheet write an essay entitled 'Why did public health improve in the nineteenth century?'

A   Health improved because of better doctors and medicines:

For
- doctors had discovered how to protect people from smallpox
- doctors had better equipment such as thermometers and stethoscopes
- there were plenty of medicines for people to try
- there were a few women doctors by 1900
- from the 1860s doctors understood what caused diseases.

Against
- vaccination against smallpox was not compulsory for most of the century and many people refused vaccination
- new equipment was good for diagnosis but not for curing illness
- the reason why people bought medicines was that doctors could not cure illnesses!
- men had not wanted women doctors and were still hostile to them.

B   Health improved because of scientific discoveries, especially germ theory:

For
- microscopes and other equipment led to new discoveries
- doctors began to use germ theory to help patients, for example, Lister's development of antiseptics
- without germ theory public health reforms would probably not have been accepted
- without germ theory there would have been no way to develop effective cures and treatments
- anaesthetics saved many people from pain.

Against
- understanding diseases was important but there was still no way to prevent many diseases spreading
- surgeons could not operate on the heart and other organs
- patients who lost a lot of blood could not be given a transfusion
- public health reforms made more difference to people's lives in the short term than did scientific discoveries.

C   Health improved because of public health reforms:

For
- fresh water, sewerage stopped the spread of many diseases
- drier, airier housing was better for health
- diet improved as laws stopped shopkeepers adulterating food
- better nutrition meant that children had more resistance to diseases.

Against
- it was a long time before these reforms were introduced and even then they did little to help the poor
- it was germ theory that led to many of the public health reforms
- there were still outbreaks of many diseases such as typhoid.

Health jigsaw 1900

What medical care was provided for Blake Sullivan when he was wounded?

Use this worksheet to help you answer question 1 on page 151.

1. Circle all those aspects of medical care that would not have been available in the Boer War in 1899.
2. Think about which aspects of medical care had been developed as a result of war.

Medical progress in the First World War

Use this worksheet for the Task on page 153. The sentences below can be used as the basis for your answer to the essay question 'The First World War helped more than it hindered developments in medicine.'

Refer to the sources on pages 150–153 to help you.

■ Before the First World War doctors were able to ...

_____

_____

_____

■ Surgeons faced three fundamental problems ...

_____

_____

_____

■ The war and the huge number of casualties forced developments in the careers of ...

_____

_____

_____

■ It can be argued that the First World War hindered the development of surgery techniques ...

_____

_____

_____

■ There were without doubt three main areas of rapid improvement ...

_____

_____

_____

■ War improved surgery for a number of reasons. They have been summarised by Heneage Ogilvy ...

_____

_____

_____

■ However, it is also important to point out the disadvantages of the impact of the war on medicine. The greatest of these was ...

_____

_____

_____

■ On balance ...

_____

_____

_____

The fight against infection

During the nineteenth century doctors and scientists discovered the causes of many illnesses and infectious diseases. They identified the bacteria and started two lines of research in the hope that they would eventually be able to prevent and cure those diseases.

Line 1: Prevention

Pasteur began the first line of research with his germ theory

Koch then identified the bacteria which caused specific diseases.

Using Koch's methods the bacteria causing other diseases were quickly discovered.

Pasteur discovered ways of using weakened forms of bacteria to give the body immunity

Following Pasteur other vaccines were developed although very slowly.

In 1906 Calmette and Guerin discovered a vaccine against tuberculosis

In 1913 Behring perfected a diphtheria vaccine.

Line 2: Cure

Koch set off the line of research by discovering that he could stain certain bacteria

Paul Ehrlich searched for a stain that would also kill the bacteria.

At first this line of research met with little success. It seemed to be hoping for the impossible. But after many patient experiments...

It works! 606 works!

Following Ehrlich, others continued the search for magic bullets.

The development of penicillin

Use this worksheet to help record which factors were of most importance at each stage of the development of penicillin. This will help you answer question 3 of the Task on page 159.

FACTORS								
	Government	Scientific experiment	Industry	Communications	War	Chance	Technology	Individuals
1928 Fleming discovers mould has killed germs								
1929 Fleming writes articles about penicillin								
1937 Florey and Chain begin research in Oxford on penicillin after reading article by Fleming								
1940 Experiment with mice								
1941 Penicillin first tested on a human being in Oxford								
1942 US and British governments co-operate to fund production of penicillin								
1944 Enough penicillin to treat all the allied forces wounded in the D-Day invasion of Europe								

STAGES

Fleming and the discovery of penicillin

This worksheet provides an account by Howard Florey of the discovery of penicillin.

■ TASK

Read through the source and highlight in different colours any references to the factors of:

- ■ individuals
- ■ technology
- ■ chance
- ■ war
- ■ industry
- ■ scientific experiment
- ■ government

which affected the development of penicillin.

SOURCE: H. Florey, 'Penicillin: a survey', *British Medical Journal*, 1944, II, pp. 169–171. Reprinted in *Science, Technology and Everyday Life*: Volume 1, edited by G.K. Roberts (1988)

The chemotherapeutic properties of penicillin were discovered in 1940, but before this there was a long history which for convenience can be divided into stages. (1) The discovery of naturally occurring antibacterial substances – or antibiotics, as they are now beginning to be called – and the early attempts to utilize them in medicine. (2) The discovery of the antibacterial substance penicillin by Alexander Fleming. (3) The discovery of its chemotherapeutic properties at Oxford. (4) The stage of development in which we are at present [1944], which consists of three interrelated lines of research – namely, (i) exploration of methods for mass-producing penicillin by the growth of the mould *Penicillium notatum*; (ii) investigation of the chemical structure of penicillin with the hope that it may eventually be synthesized by chemical means; and (iii) the clinical exploitation of the known properties of penicillin.

Stage 1

We have to go back to 1877 for the first observation of a naturally produced antibacterial substance. In that year Pasteur and Joubert described how when common air bacteria contaminated flasks of broth containing the bacillus of anthrax the growth of the anthrax bacillus was stopped. That phenomenon was probably the first observation that one organism may produce a chemical substance – or antibiotic – which is capable of stopping the growth of another, though Pasteur did not realize its true significance.

Stage 2

In 1928 Fleming was studying the staphylococcus. One day he examined and then put aside on his bench a plate on which colonies of the staphylococcus were growing. Several days later there was a colony of mould growing on one side. Fleming noticed that in the neighbourhood of the mould the colonies of staphylococci were disappearing. He recognized this as a phenomenon of interest, and subcultured the mould, which was later identified as *Penicillium notatum*. When grown on nutrient broth it was found to produce some substance which passed into the liquid. By experiments in test-tubes Fleming showed that the liquid had the property of stopping the growth of many bacteria. Fleming called the active liquid penicillin. He carried out experiments on the effect of his broth on numerous organisms in test-tubes and showed that many which can cause disease in man were affected,

although some disease-producing organisms were quite insensitive… About this time an attempt was made by Clutterbuck, Lovell, and Raistrick to extract the penicillin. They succeeded in growing the mould on a purely synthetic medium and found that the active substance could be extracted into ether when the watery medium containing penicillin was acidified. However, when they tried to concentrate the penicillin by evaporating the ether most of the activity was lost, and they concluded that penicillin was 'extremely labile'.

… as the result of both Fleming's and Clutterbuck, Lovell, and Raistrick's work the conclusion had been reached that penicillin was an unstable substance and therefore unlikely to have any practical value in medicine.

Stage 3

Stage 3 deals with the work done at Oxford. My own interest in the phenomena of bacterial inhibition began in the 1920s. Since 1929, at first alone and later with collaborators, work had been in progress, but it was not till 1938 that Dr Chain, a biochemist, and I prepared a plan for the systematic study of some of the naturally produced antibacterial substances. Miss Schoental obtained three antibacterial products from *Bacillus pyocyaneus*, which all proved to be very toxic, but fortunately the results with penicillin turned out rather differently.

The body of work done by this team in the next two years produced a single end-result – penicillin as a proved chemotherapeutic drug.

The fact that penicillin is a very powerful antibacterial agent would not by itself differentiate it from a number of other mould products or from some of the familiar chemical antiseptics. But whereas nearly all such substances are quite toxic to body tissues, even concentrated extracts of penicillin had practically no poisonous action on animals. It was further shown that individual body cells, such as the white cells of the blood, were unaffected by concentrations many hundreds of times greater than those necessary to stop the growth of sensitive organisms.

When administered to an infected animal or man in sufficient quantity penicillin stops the growth of the germs, thus giving the white blood cells in particular, and possibly other defence mechanisms, the opportunity effectively to attack and destroy them.

The position at which we had now arrived was that we had in our hands a substance which combined very low toxicity to animals with a very powerful action against disease-producing bacteria. We knew a good deal about its fundamental behaviour in the animal body. The most important step had now been reached – we had still to learn whether it would cure disease in animals and man.

The following experiments demonstrated that penicillin belongs to the class of true chemotherapeutic agents. So far as the use of penicillin in medicine is concerned this was the crucial discovery. Such experiments are carried out in the following way. Mice are injected with bacteria such as streptococci and staphylococci so that they will certainly die from the infection within one or at most two days. To show that a substance suspected of having chemotherapeutic properties is active it is necessary to secure survival of a substantial number of mice which would otherwise certainly die. In the case of penicillin this was accomplished by injecting some penicillin under the skins of the infected animals every three hours for several days. The groups of treated mice survived almost without exception, while the untreated mice all died. These first experiments indicated without any doubt that penicillin belonged to that rare class of drugs which can be used as chemotherapeutic agents.

From this demonstration it appeared that penicillin was likely to have very great potentialities in the field of human medicine. Penicillin at that time was extremely difficult to produce in substantial quantities, so that some time passed before we were able to show its powers on man. We again have to thank Dr Heatley and his assistants for unremitting work in producing in the laboratory enough penicillin for the first injections in man. Even after months of work we could treat only six cases of severe infection, but the results were most promising.

The first human patients were treated in the winter and spring of 1940–1, at the time of the worst bombing of England. It seemed improbable that much headway could be made in getting large-scale production started in this country. In these circumstances Dr Heatley and

Medicine & Health Through Time

I went to America, which was not then at war, to ask them whether they could put some of their great resources into the production of penicillin, so that more extensive clinical trials could be carried out. We were extremely fortunate in coming into contact with Dr Coghill, Director of the Fermentation Division of the Department of Agriculture's excellent research laboratory at Peoria, in Illinois. The work which he and his colleagues have done … has played an important part in the large-scale production of penicillin.

While this work was being initiated in America, enough material was made in Oxford and by Imperial Chemical Industries to enable some eighteen patients with severe infections, most of them caused by the staphylococcus, to be treated. These results were again of such great promise that any effort to produce the drug on a really large scale was clearly worth while. This was more so since certain of the bacteria susceptible to penicillin cause some of the most common and universal infections, including those of war wounds.

Stage 4

From that time the work branched in three directions. First, it was clear that it would be very desirable to make the substance synthetically by chemical procedures without the intervention of the mould. Work is now proceeding along those lines in Oxford, where Dr Chain and Dr Abraham are collaborating with Sir Robert Robinson and his colleagues, and elsewhere, both in this country and in America, hundreds of chemists are engaged on this important problem.

The second, and more immediately practicable line, has been to increase the manufacture by means of the mould to a really large scale. This has involved a large number of intricate technical problems, which have been tackled along different lines by the various commercial firms, both in this country and in America. As a result of their efforts penicillin can now be issued by the kilogramme, although, of course, the supplies still fall lamentably short of the demand.

The third line has been to explore further the use of penicillin as a curative agent. There are two possible ways of using penicillin. First, it can be injected into the muscles or veins so that it is carried around in the circulation to the parts which are being attacked by the infecting bacteria. This method is obligatory in the more serious and widespread diseases such as pneumonia, diseases of the bones, and septicaemia, where the diseased tissues cannot be reached by any other means. At the present time a great deal of thought and study is being given to the problem of war wounds and how best to utilize penicillin, both locally and generally, for their treatment.

The increasing supplies of penicillin now available permit of extensive explorations of its use in many diseases. Perhaps the most striking recent addition to knowledge is that of the Americans, who have discovered that penicillin is apparently effective in treating syphilis. Another excellent development since larger supplies have become available is that penicillin can now be given as a preventive instead of as a last resort. In battle casualties especially, the effort is being made to prevent serious sepsis from developing by giving penicillin at a very early stage.

Factors affecting infant mortality 1900–1945 (i)

Tick the factors which are identified by each explanation. Some explanations may identify more than one problem.

FACTORS

EXPLANATIONS OF INFANT MORTALITY	Poor parenting skills	Poor housing	Poor sanitation	Unhealthy lifestyle	Diet	Lack of education	Other (specify)
Diarrhoea caught from germs was the main cause of death of young babies. Other infectious diseases (see page 115) were also very serious.							
Infant mortality was higher in poor families, who were living in insanitary and badly ventilated housing, or eating a poor diet.							
'Infant mortality increases in proportion to adult women taking jobs in factories or farming.' *John Simon 1890*							
'Cold is a prolific cause of infant mortality.' *Birmingham Medical Officer of Health 1893*							
'Milk given to children often comes from cows in the most filthy condition. The milkers are filthy and their vessels often dirty.' (Bottle feeding was increasingly popular at this time.) *Parliament's Committee on Physical Deterioration 1904*							
'Babies are given comforters (dummies) dipped in dirty milk. They fall on the floor. They are never cleaned except on a dirty apron. They are full of germs.' *Newman's report, Infant Mortality*							
'Overcrowded housing is the most important contribution to the spread of preventable disease.' *Sir Thomas Crawford 1890*							
'On no account must a baby sleep in bed with its mother because the mother is in danger of rolling over and smothering the baby.' *Health visitor's advice 1910*							

Factors affecting infant mortality 1900 – 1945 (ii)

1. In column 1 list the factors which led to high infant mortality.
2. In column 2 use Sources 3–10 on pages 160–162 to note how and when these problems were tackled.

Factors causing high infant mortality at the turn of the century	How and when these problems were tackled

Why did infant mortality decline so rapidly from 1900 to 1945?

Use this worksheet for the Task on page 162. The sentences below provide an outline for your essay.

■ During the nineteenth century infant mortality was ...

_____

_____

_____

■ After 1900 infant mortality started to ...

_____

_____

_____

■ To explain why this happened it is necessary to look at how factors causing infant mortality were tackled. The most important factors causing infant mortality were ...

_____

_____

_____

■ Other important factors included ...

_____

_____

_____

■ Various governments encouraged change by ...

_____

_____

_____

■ People themselves also helped by becoming more aware of ...

_____

_____

_____

■ The contribution of science was ...

_____

_____

_____

■ The most important reasons for the decline of infant mortality between 1900 and 1945 were ...

_____

_____

_____

The impact of the Second World War on medicine and health in Britain

Use this worksheet for the Task on page 163.

Development	How it improved health	How the war caused this development	Would it have happened without the war? Yes, no, possibly. Explain your choice
Surgery: improved blood transfusion			
Surgery: improved skin grafts			
Rationing			
Health education posters and campaigns			
Diphtheria immunisation campaign			
The first antibiotic drug			
Evacuation			
Government decision to provide a NHS			

Why did people oppose the National Health Service?

Use this worksheet to help with the Activity on page 168. Record the main arguments against the introduction of the NHS by an opponent, and the main arguments put forward by Nye Bevan in its favour.

Opposition	Nye Bevan

How did the National Health Service change health care in Britain after 1948?

Use this worksheet to help you with the Task on page 169. Refer to the information on pages 164–169.

■ Before 1948 most health care was provided by . . .

_____

_____

_____

_____

■ After 1948 it was . . .

_____

_____

_____

_____

■ This affected various aspects of health care, for example going to the doctor.

■ Before 1948 this involved . . .

_____

_____

_____

_____

■ After 1948 it involved . . .

_____

_____

_____

_____

■ Hospital care also changed. In the 1930s hospitals had . . .

_____

_____

_____

_____

■ After 1948 they . . .

_____

_____

_____

_____

■ The most important changes brought about by the NHS were . . .

_____

_____

_____

Continuity or change: attitudes to epidemic diseases

Use this worksheet for Task 1 on page 172.

Compare AIDS with either the Black Death in the Middle Ages or cholera in the nineteenth century. An example has been filled in for you.

SIMILARITIES

AIDS	Black Death	Cholera
People looked for scapegoats to blame for the disease, such as gay people.	People looked for scapegoats to blame, for example, the Jews.	

DIFFERENCES

Medicine & Health Through Time

The war between man and microbe

This worksheet provides additional sources which show that people have not won the battle against deadly microbes.

1. From Sources 1 and 2 highlight examples of the factors:
   - war
   - communication

   which have assisted the resurgence of deadly microbes.
2. Which of the developments mentioned in Sources 1 and 2 do you think poses the greatest threat to people's health today?

SOURCE 1 Adapted from an article by journalist Steve Connor in the *Independent*, September 1995

❝ The war between man and microbe
In the 1970s medical science seemed almost triumphant. Vaccines, antibiotics and improvements in housing and diet had apparently finally beaten many of the great infectious diseases of history. The optimists could point to the total worldwide eradication of smallpox in 1977 as a result of a global vaccination campaign. The World Health Organisation predicted that, by the year 2000, polio would be the next disease to be beaten.

However, such optimism has become strangely out of place in the post-AIDS world. The sudden appearance of the HIV virus, and its rapid spread around the planet, has become one of the most alarming developments in the history of twentieth-century medicine. The emergence of other diseases, such as the Ebola virus in Zaire or the hantavirus in the US, has increased concern about the deadly infectious grenades that nature can still lob in our direction.

On top of this, bacterial diseases that were once easy to treat with antibiotics have become widely resistant to our arsenal of drugs – resistant strains of TB are now prevalent in New York City and some hospitals in Britain.

Our optimism about the power of medical progress was premature. It did not take into account the extraordinary resilience of infectious microbes. These have a remarkable ability to evolve, adapt and develop resistance to drugs in an unpredictable and dynamic fashion. It also did not take into account the accelerating spread of human populations into tropical forests and overcrowded mega-cities where people are exposed to a variety of emerging infectious agents.

The globalisation of human societies has now created the conditions where a little local difficulty can become a world pandemic. ❞

SOURCE 2 Adapted from *The Coming Plague*, 1995, by Laurie Garrett. She is describing the spread of dengue haemorrhagic fever. Dengue fever is a mosquito-carried disease which thrives in urban areas. Dengue fever had been virtually wiped out in the earlier part of the century but in the 1950s it suddenly reappeared

❝ In 1953 Manila was hit by an apparently new form of dengue in which pinpoint-sized red spots started bleeding, accompanied by shock and high fevers with convulsions and in 15 per cent of cases death. Through the 1950s and 1960s it spread through South and East Asia.

When scientists set out to reconstruct the events that led to the emergence of urban dengue haemorrhagic fever they concluded that every advance of the microbe was the direct result of human activities. In World War II massive human migrations, aerial bombing campaigns, densely populated refugee camps and the wartime disruption of all mosquito control efforts allowed an unprecedented surge in the insect population. The mosquitoes were able to use bomb craters filled with water as breeding sites. They drew blood from the millions of war victims whose homes were destroyed and no longer provided night-time protection from hungry insects. The Korean and Vietnam wars created further opportunities for mosquito breeding. By 1975 dengue was endemic in urban centres throughout South East Asia.

The surge in commercial air traffic through the 1970s allowed the spread of the disease to the slums of cities in Latin America.

The mosquito carrying the dengue-2 virus was a fully urbanised insect. It thrived only in proximity to human beings, laying its eggs in open containers of fresh water and maturing inside human shelters.

In 1985 the mosquito was carried aboard a shipment of tyres sent from Japan to Texas for retreading. The extremely aggressive mosquitoes – capable of carrying both dengue and yellow fever – quickly out-competed more timid domestic species. Within two years the mosquito was seeking human blood in the cities and towns of 17 American states. ❞

Hereford Street, Brighton

Use this worksheet to help with the Activity on page 176.

1. Label the features of back-to-back houses that were likely to cause ill health.

Artist's reconstruction of houses in Hereford Street, Brighton

2. Label the features of these new houses that help to make them healthier dwellings.

An illustration of the houses that replaced the old back-to-back
houses of Hereford Street

Is poor health the fate of all developing countries?

Use this worksheet for the Task on page 178. Record your view as to how serious a problem each category is/was for people in developing countries today and for people in nineteenth-century Britain. Remember to explain your reasons.

Nineteenth-century Britain   **Developing nations today**

DISEASE

DIET

INEQUALITY

WAR

COMMUNICATIONS

EDUCATION

UNSAFE OR
INAPPROPRIATE
DRUGS

INFANT
MORTALITY

Twentieth-century medicine: conclusions

Use this worksheet to help you answer the questions in Task 1 on page 179.

Examples of medicine:	war	religion	government	science and technology	trade and communications	chance	individual genius
a) getting slowly or gradually better							
b) getting better very quickly							
c) staying the same							
d) getting slowly worse							
e) getting rapidly worse							

Factors which caused change or continuity

Medicine & Health Through Time

Progress in the twentieth century

Use this worksheet for your answer to question 3 of Task 1 on page 179.

■ Introductory statement

_____

_____

_____

_____

_____

■ a) understanding of disease

_____

_____

_____

_____

_____

■ b) improving treatments

_____

_____

_____

_____

_____

■ c) improving ordinary people's health

_____

_____

_____

_____

_____

■ d) public health

_____

_____

_____

_____

_____

■ Conclusion

_____

_____

_____

_____

_____

Twentieth-century medicine: conclusions

Use this worksheet for question 1 of Task 2 on page 179.

Medicine & Health Through Time © JOHN MURRAY

Doctors' role in improving health

Use this worksheet to help you answer question 3 on page 180.

How significant do you think the contribution of doctors has been in improving medicine and health in the twentieth century? Use the points below to make notes which will help you plan and structure your answer.

Paragraph 1 – Introduction
■ What you think the question means. Consider what other factors were important in the developments in medicine and health.

Paragraph 2 – How doctors' roles have changed. You could look at:
■ their role in the 1930s
■ their involvement in the introduction of the NHS – opposition and support
■ the role of the GP.

Paragraph 3 – How important other factors have been and how doctors have contributed to these:
■ scientific research
■ the importance of technology
■ the role of public health in improving standards of health.

Paragraph 4 – Your conclusion as to how important the contribution of doctors has been.

Methods of treatment through time

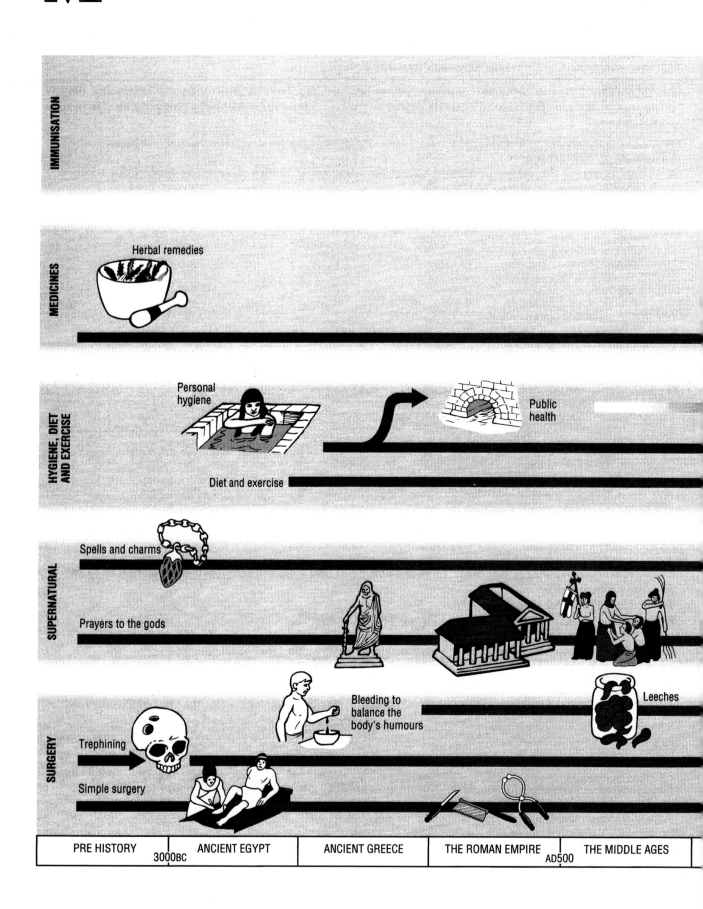

IMMUNISATION

MEDICINES

Herbal remedies

HYGIENE, DIET AND EXERCISE

Personal hygiene

Public health

Diet and exercise

SUPERNATURAL

Spells and charms

Prayers to the gods

SURGERY

Trephining

Simple surgery

Bleeding to balance the body's humours

Leeches

PRE HISTORY	ANCIENT EGYPT	ANCIENT GREECE	THE ROMAN EMPIRE	THE MIDDLE AGES
3000BC			AD500	

Medicine & Health Through Time

© JOHN MURRAY

1700s
Smallpox inoculation
Smallpox vaccination
1798
1880s
Other vaccinations
Anti-toxins

Patent medicines
RHUBARB REMEDY
Chemical drugs
1890s
ASPIRIN
1920s
1940s
Antibiotics
PENICILLIN
SULPHONAMIDES

1875 PUBLIC HEALTH ACT

ABRACADABRA

1940s
plastic surgery
1960s
transplants
1980s
keyhole surgery
Increasingly complex surgery
1840s
Anaesthetics
1860s
Antisepsis
1890s
X-rays
1914
Blood transfusion

THE MEDICAL RENAISSANCE
1750
1750–1900
1900
THE TWENTIETH CENTURY

Factor analysis

Medicine & Health Through Time

Factors affecting the history of health and medicine

Use this worksheet to record your answers to the questions on page 187.

Using different colours, circle the factors which you think have been the most important in the history of medicine for:
- maintaining continuity
- causing change.

Factor	Did this factor lead to change or to continuity?	List two ways that this factor affected the history of medicine.
		1. 2.
		1. 2.
		1. 2.
		1. 2.
		1. 2.
		1. 2.
		1. 2.
		1. 2.

Factor 3: War

Use this worksheet to help you tackle the Sources 1–5 on pages 192–193.

1. List as many examples as you can of war changing medicine for the better.

_____

_____

_____

2. List as many examples as you can of war preventing change in medicine.

_____

_____

_____

3. Has war done more to change medicine for the better or to stop change in medicine? Explain the reasons for your answer.

_____

_____

_____

4. In which periods has war had the greatest effect on the development of medicine? Give examples of these effects.

_____

_____

_____

5. Has war caused change by itself or has it worked together with other factors? Use one example to explain your answer.

_____

_____

_____

6. How important has war been in the development of medicine and health?

■ Very important

_____

_____

_____

■ Important

_____

_____

_____

■ Not very important

_____

_____

_____

Medicine & Health Through Time © JOHN MURRAY

The role of individuals (i)

The role of individuals (ii)

Use this worksheet to answer questions 3 and 4 on page 194.

GALEN   VESALIUS   JENNER
                        SIMPSON KOCH

PREHISTORY	ANCIENT EGYPT	ANCIENT GREECE	THE ROMAN EMPIRE	THE MIDDLE AGES	THE MEDICAL RENAISSANCE	1750–1900	THE TWENTIETH CENTURY

3000BC   AD500   AD1750   AD1900
                                 AVICENNA   PARÉ   CHADWICK NIGHTINGALE

The role of individuals (iii)

Medicine & Health Through Time

How did different factors work together to produce change in the Medical Renaissance?

CHANGE IN RELIGIOUS
BELIEFS AND
ATTITUDES
All kinds of ideas were
being challenged, as was
the power of the Catholic
Church itself. Challenging
Galen's ideas was easier
when religion was being
questioned

INDIVIDUAL GENIUS
Vesalius, Paré and Harvey were
intelligent and observant
individuals

COMMUNICATIONS
The new invention of printing
spread ideas quickly so that
doctors learned from each
other. Doctors also learned
from scientific artists

WHY
were there medical
discoveries
at the time of the
Renaissance?

WAR AND CHANCE
When Paré ran out of oil
he tried a new treatment
which turned out to be
more successful

SCIENCE AND TECHNOLOGY
Discoveries inspired more
new ideas. New machines
were being invented. Harvey
believed the heart pumped
blood in the same way as
other pumps pumped water

How did different factors work together to beat killer diseases?

Use this worksheet to complete Task 2 on page 197.

How factors worked together to beat the killer diseases of the nineteenth century

Medicine & Health Through Time © JOHN MURRAY

How did different factors work together to prevent change?

Use this worksheet to answer question 1 on page 198.

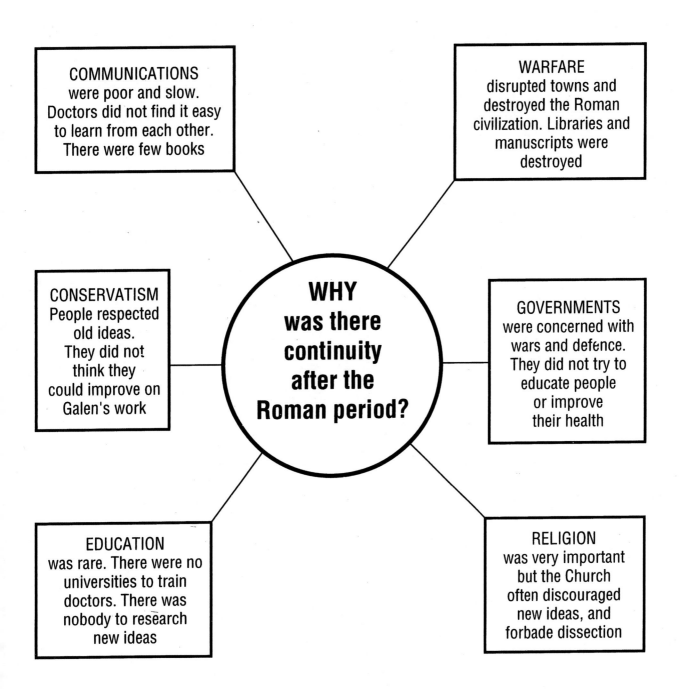

COMMUNICATIONS
were poor and slow.
Doctors did not find it easy
to learn from each other.
There were few books

WARFARE
disrupted towns and
destroyed the Roman
civilization. Libraries and
manuscripts were
destroyed

CONSERVATISM
People respected
old ideas.
They did not
think they
could improve on
Galen's work

WHY
was there
continuity
after the
Roman period?

GOVERNMENTS
were concerned with
wars and defence.
They did not try to
educate people
or improve
their health

EDUCATION
was rare. There were no
universities to train
doctors. There was
nobody to research
new ideas

RELIGION
was very important
but the Church
often discouraged
new ideas, and
forbade dissection

Women as doctors

Use this worksheet to help you answer Task 2 on page 202.

Look at the page references on the timeline. Add your own notes to the right of the timeline to build up a picture of women's role as doctors. Then in your own exercise book answer these questions:

1. Was there a time when women could not become doctors?
2. Why were women unable to become doctors then?
3. Earlier in history some women did become doctors. Was it unusual for women to become doctors in those times?
4. In the twentieth century it has become easier for women to become doctors. Why?
5. Are there any reasons why it is still difficult for women to become doctors?

Pages

18 Source 5	Egypt
29 Source 3	Greece
41	Rome
69	Medieval
92–93	1500s
104–105	1700s
124–125	1800s

Medicine & Health Through Time   © JOHN MURRAY

The history of hospitals

Use this worksheet to help you answer Task 2 on page 205.

Look at the page references on the timeline. Add your own notes to the right of the timeline to build up a picture of the development of hospitals.

Pages

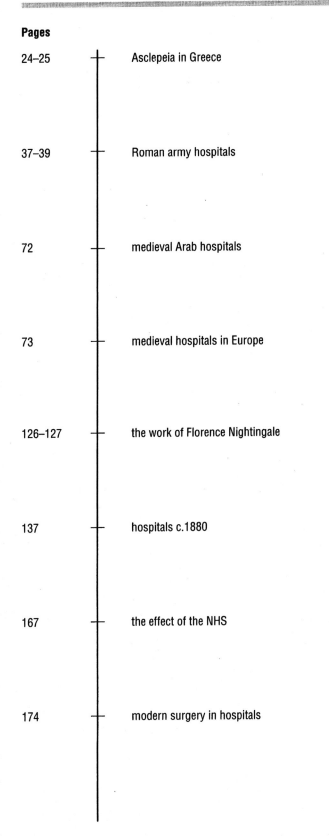

24–25   Asclepeia in Greece

37–39   Roman army hospitals

72   medieval Arab hospitals

73   medieval hospitals in Europe

126–127   the work of Florence Nightingale

137   hospitals c.1880

167   the effect of the NHS

174   modern surgery in hospitals

The consequences of germ theory

Use this worksheet to answer question 4 of the Task on page 206.

Write an essay titled 'Why was germ theory a turning point in the history of medicine?' You can use these sentences to begin each paragraph of your essay but first you will have to complete them!

■ Germ theory was a vital turning point. Before Pasteur's discovery doctors did not understand what caused disease. After his discovery . . .

_____
_____
_____
_____
_____

■ Germ theory led to the development of vaccines against . . .

_____
_____
_____
_____
_____

■ Germ theory also helped surgeons because . . .

_____
_____
_____
_____
_____

■ Public health also improved after Pasteur's discovery because . . .

_____
_____
_____
_____

■ As a result of all these changes life expectancy began to increase . . .

_____
_____
_____
_____

APPENDIX: USING THIS TEACHERS' RESOURCE BOOK ALONGSIDE MEDICINE FOR EDEXCEL

In 2001 SHP produced a new edition of *Medicine and Health Through Time* targeted at the Edexcel GCSE specification. Most of this Teachers' Resource Book can be used with minimal adaptation to support the Edexcel edition. This short appendix therefore

- summarises the main features of the Edexcel edition
- explains how the worksheets in this Teachers' Resource Book can be used with *Medicine for Edexcel* including what adaptation may be needed.

Features of *Medicine for Edexcel*

- **Chapters 1–4** cover most of the same chronological content as the first five chapters of the first edition; they have been reorganised into four chapters to reflect the way the Edexcel specification is structured chronologically. Content not required by Edexcel (for example the prehistoric period) has been cut.

- **Chapter 1** (3000BC–AD1350): Coverage of Egypt, Greece and Rome has been abridged since it is not a core topic for Edexcel. For example, rather than making detailed reference to who provided medical care in each period, we have simply summarised the key points on page 7. Key ideas have been presented more concisely wherever possible – for example the theory of the four Humours on page 17.

- **Chapter 2** (1350–1750) combines the medieval period and the Renaissance period which were two chapters in the first edition.

- The order of the topics in **Chapter 3** (1750–1900) has been changed to reflect the Edexcel specification and more summaries have been added, e.g. on pages 94–95. Florence Nightingale has been covered in more depth.

- **Chapter 4** (the twentieth century) has been extensively revised and includes new material on Marie Curie (pages 146–147) and DNA (pages 148–151) which are central topics in Edexcel. The DNA material aims to be as non-scientific as possible and to focus on the historical issue of why the breakthroughs happened when they did.

- **Chapter 5** (explaining change and continuity) is more extensive than in the first edition and includes enquiries into the Edexcel optional themes (hospitals and surgery). It also reviews material on those themes which have been added to the earlier chapters of the book. The material on training and hospitals (see pages 82–87, 128–129 and 172–173) is mostly new.

- **Factors:** The analysis of factors causing change has been revised to reflect Edexcel's distinctive approach. For example, the focus is on attitudes rather than on religion.

- New **summaries** highlighting key questions required for the Edexcel specification have been added. For example, there are summaries on public health (pages 42–43); medieval medicine (pages 45–46); the Renaissance (pages 88–89); reasons for change (page 93); and recent changes in methods of treatment (page 145).

- **Key individual:** This is a new feature to reflect the Edexcel emphasis on named individuals. For example, key individual summaries have been added on Pasteur (page 105), Chadwick (pages 114–115), and Lister (pages 122 and 134–135).

- **Exam practice:** Two past exam papers have been included to provide exam practice – pages 73–75 on the Plague; and pages 136–139 on Florence Nightingale.

HOW TO USE THE WORKSHEETS IN THIS TRB WITH MEDICINE FOR EDEXCEL

Those worksheets not mentioned have no direct application to *Medicine for Edexcel*.

Worksheets	TRB pages for teachers' notes	Supports *Medicine for Edexcel* pages	Notes N.B. In most cases the page number referred to on each worksheet will need changing to the page number in column 3.
1–4	5–6	2–3	Omit prehistoric material from activities as not required for Edexcel specification
9–10	8	6–9	Use unchanged
11	8–9	12	Questions 3 and 4 transposed
12	9	N/A	Could be used as an additional activity
15	11–12	23–25	Use unchanged
16	12	16	Use unchanged
17	12	27–29	Use unchanged
18	12	30–31	Could be used as an additional activity
19	12	14–34	Could be used as an additional activity
22–23	13	32–33	Use unchanged
24	13	N/A	Could be used as an additional summary
25–27	13	35–36	Use unchanged
29–31	14–15	48–51	Use unchanged
32	15	86	Use to label features of hospital treatments
33	15	45–46	Could be used as an additional activity
34	17	60–61	Could be used as an additional activity
35	17–18	64–65	Could use the idea. However, the sequence of boxes and headings differs from the Students' Book
37	19	90	Use unchanged
38	19	80–81, 91	Use unchanged
39	19	N/A	Could be used as an additional summary
40	19	Summarises 57–90	Could be used as an additional revision activity
41	20	Extends 94–95	Students can record details as they work on Chapter 3
42	20	140	Could be used as an additional activity
45–46	21	96–99	Could be used as an additional activity
47–48	21	124–125	Use unchanged
49–50	22	132–135	Use by amending heading in Worksheet 50 from Religion to Attitudes and Beliefs
51	22	130–131	Use unchanged
52	22	100–101	Use unchanged
53	22	101	Use but step 6 refers to p. 102
54–55	22	102	Use unchanged
56–57	22	104	Use unchanged
58	23	104	Use unchanged with Source 7
59	23	105	Use unchanged with obituary activity

Worksheets	TRB pages for teachers' notes	Supports *Medicine for Edexcel* pages	Notes N.B. In most cases the page number referred to on each worksheet will need changing to the page number in column 3.
60	23	116	Use unchanged
61	23	116–118	Use by amending Religion to Attitudes and Beliefs
62	23	119–121	Use with Activity 2, p. 121
63	23	119–121	Use with Task on p. 121
64	23	106	Use unchanged
65–66	23–24	106–107	Use unchanged
67	24	110	Use unchanged
68–70	24	112	Use unchanged
71	24	113	Use unchanged
72–73	24	142	Use unchanged
74	24	142	Use unchanged
76	26	152–153, 175	This worksheet can be used as an additional revision task
77	26	156	Use unchanged
78–79	26	158–161	Use unchanged
80	27	170–171	Could be used as extension material
82	27	175	Source 4 on p. 175 now relates to war in general, not just World War Two
83–84	27	168–169	Use unchanged
87	28	162–163	Use unchanged
88	28	N/A	This material could be used for research
89–90	28–29	Summarises Chapter 4	Could be used as free-standing worksheets
92	29	N/A	Could be used as an additional activity
93	30	178–179	Use unchanged
94–95	30	182–183	Use unchanged
96	31	188–189	Could be used as an additional activity
97–99	31	190	Use unchanged
100–102	31–32	192–193	Use unchanged
104	32	202–203	Can be used to build up additional information on hospitals but all page numbers need changing – see contents list
105	32	100–105	Use unchanged